*This book is dedicated to my father,*
*Dr. Daniel C. Gramzow—the seed*
*that inspired its growth.*
*It was a privilege to have been raised by you,*
*loved by you, and quite simply ...*
*to have known you.*

# Common Stones

A glimpse into several different worlds, in an effort
to become more acquainted with our own

## ALICIA M. SMITH

Inspiring Voices·

In some instances, the author condensed time, changed the names of characters
or locations, or wrote the story "to the best of the interviewee's recollection."

Inspiring Voices books may be ordered through booksellers or by contacting:

Inspiring Voices
1663 Liberty Drive
Bloomington, IN 47403
www.inspiringvoices.com
1 (866) 697-5313

ISBN: 978-1-4624-1164-1 (sc)
ISBN: 978-1-4624-1163-4 (e)

Library of Congress Control Number: 2015916606

Print information available on the last page.

Inspiring Voices rev. date: 12/3/2015

# PRAISE FOR *COMMON STONES*

"The essays themselves are tightly paced and engaging.....Inspirational without being patronizing; a well-organized collection."

*–Kirkus Reviews*

*Common Stones* is anything but common and is so much more than just another story. As I read this book I almost felt like I was there, within the individual stories. Stories of overcoming steep odds and the power of God to move mountains in our lives if we simply let Him. As you read and absorb the different events brought about by life as it happened to each person, you cannot help but come away with an important realization. It is not the pain, nor the negative circumstance that matters in the end—it is what you choose to do with these things that really matters. I recommend this book to anyone of any age—you are never too old or too young to be inspired and touched by grace.

*–Greg Holt, Christian Blogger/Publisher,* Inspirational Christian Blogs & The Olive Branch Report

*Common Stones* blew me away. So many details were relevant in the plot(s) and around the edges. So many real people and places. Mostly, it was powerful. I couldn't put it down. One minute I was in tears recalling so many people who need to read these words, but also because I was wishing I had read this ten years ago. Alicia Smith's conclusions drove right to the core—not "preachy" and overly theological, but very profound. She spoke candidly about pain, trials and overcoming from a Godly perspective. *Common Stones* simply made my day. I loved it! In fact, it's the best book I have read in some time.

*–Dale Robble, Senior Pastor, Highland Park Church, Nashville, TN*

# ACKNOWLEDGEMENTS

*To My Heavenly Father:* I can't help but feel that this book has very little to do with me and my efforts. You, above all else, provided every bit of knowledge, skill, passion, and motivation. At times I literally felt as if You were physically at the keyboard as opposed to me. My eternal appreciation for Your constant presence, guidance, grace, and love. You are all that is good in this world.

*To My Interviewees ~ Our Inspirational Leaders:* In making the decision to share your most delicate moments, you took a colossal chance on me, not having a single concrete example of my work or success. Your decision to join me on the *Common Stones* journey was the very definition of faith—faith that I would cherish and present your words in their most authentic light. You made this decision simply with the common goal to help others. Pure selflessness and generosity. You have touched my life beyond the words of this book, each of you holding a very special place in my heart. I hope to always call you my friends.

*To My Husband, Ryan:* You believed in me when I didn't; you gave me courage when there was none; and you shower me every single day with the purest love a person can provide. You and me. Side-by-side. Tomorrow's surprises will never overtake us. ~ People wonder if God exists. My dad would say that after looking in the mirror, at the miraculous and complex creation of human life that is displayed within our reflection, how could one *not* believe in God? I have always loved the simplicity of that perspective. But the truth is, I only need to look at you. There is no greater reminder of God's existence.

*To Mom and Dad:* You both taught me how to nurture and value my greatest gift in this life—my faith in God. I will never be able to repay you for this, but I promise to live that faith as best I can, attempting to do the same for others that you have done for me. You were/are not only my parents, but my mentors ... my guideposts. I never want to know where I would be without you.

*To My Dear Sisters:* First of all, thank you for letting me share moments that provoke us to crumble just through their memory. Hopefully, those pages weren't only a reminder of the pain, but also of the blessings. ~ This world never promises a safety net, yet somehow I got lucky. I've always known that no matter where I was or what endeavor I was embarking upon, there were six supportive arms ready to hold me up, urge me onward, or catch me when needed. Thank you for your constant encouragement and what feels like endless faith in who I am and what I do.

*To My Friends and other Family Members:* The overwhelming support and positivity you have given me cannot be estimated or exceeded. I'm a better person, having each of you by my side.

*To My Editors:* Susan Malone, Dr. Melanie Gramzow, Annie Schenck, Dr. Shaefer Spires, and the American Christian Writers group, you were/are phenomenal, and all offered crucial guidance/wisdom as to *Common Stones'* progression. Candice Belanger, also one of my editors and dear friends, passed away March 1, 2015; her skill was invaluable, her heart/passion provided bottomless inspiration, and her friendship—irreplaceable. *I miss you every day, Candice.*

> *Without the efforts of every single one of the individuals*
> *above,* Common Stones *would not exist. I only hope*
> *and pray that you are proud of its outcome;*
> *it is as much yours as it is mine.*
> *All of my love, gratitude, and admiration ....*

# CONTENTS

# CHAPTER 1

## The Common Thread

*"We all live with the objective of being happy; our*
*lives are all different and yet the same."*
*~Anne Frank*

*Y*ou would think I'd be used to this by now. Apparently not. I struggled to determine where I was, my eyes straining to decipher the shadows cast by the alarm clock's soft glow. *The guest room. I'm home. Groundhog Day.* A deep breath inflated my chest while my head found its way to my hands. *Not again.*

When was this going to stop? When would it stop hurting? And dear Lord, when would the repair men let me and my husband live on the first floor again! On the lower level of our townhouse, an uninsulated pipe decided to freeze and rupture, spewing water in various directions. Every square inch of flooring needed to be replaced. It had been three long weeks of seclusion on the small second floor—sleeping in the guest room, relocating my closet to the bathtub, and "the kitchen" consisting of only a miniature fridge in the adjacent office. But our new accommodations were just the icing on the cake.

My mind was determined to evade rest. The flashbacks returned, night after night. I ran my fingers through my hair and squeezed my eyes tightly, determined to shut their water off, just as we had for that detestable pipe downstairs. *There must be someone I can talk to. Someone who knows what this feels like.* But was there? Would anyone

1

understand? *Tell me how to do this! Tell me how to heal! Tell me how to just ... get by.* I needed to talk to someone. More importantly, I needed to hear someone tell me *their* story.

\* \* \*

Every once in a while I catch myself wishing I knew people's experiences, or even their descriptive thoughts. Perhaps you've eased yourself into a chair at a coffee shop, distracted by all the commotion swirling around, and imagined scenarios of other people's lives. Occasionally I've experienced strangers striking up an impromptu conversation after a curious glance at the book I was reading. Once, sitting at a large community table in Starbucks, I shared a moment with a man on his ninetieth birthday. Upon settling in at the head of the table, he drank his tea while reading the morning newspaper, completely content with the little things in life. This precious man had never experienced being a hospital patient in his entire life. Astonishing and extremely celebratory. I often walk away from these encounters with another perspective that I never anticipated receiving during a work session with my morning java.

\* \* \*

We all have a common thread, our own stories, our own soundtracks that represent our lives. We struggle with a desperate hope to persevere. We want to be needed, to be appreciated for our talents, our passions, and our characteristics—what we bring to the table, unique from everyone else on this planet. We want to fulfill some type of purpose, whatever that may be. These threads create not only our own patch of tapestry, but combined, become a bigger idea, a masterpiece linking each of us. Not a single thread can be replaced. It may dull or endure wear and tear, but it maintains its purpose. It supports the others, creating a one-of-a-kind symphony of intention.

What about our stepping stones? The ones that stabilize our

shaky ground? The ones that support us above our rivers and valleys? The ones that teach us how and where to stand? Do we share any common stones? If so, what are they and why do we absolutely need them to reach higher ground? Why stand by, observing another's thirst for water, when you've already drank from the well that they seek? The steps to that well have been charted. Why not share them? Isn't that what makes life interesting—living our stories and sharing our moments with others, good and bad? Diving into the anecdotes that have made people who they are? Learning from each other's experiences and stepping stones, feeling connected in some way and not so alone in a world that at times leaves us feeling cornered and helpless?

The upcoming pages offer just that—a compilation of stories, stories that will hopefully produce even an ounce of inspiration, healing, and hope. This began as a personal research project, plunging into excerpts from people's lives to discover how *they* made it through. How they carried on. How they learned to keep moving, despite life's pitfalls. These testimonies are one-hundred-percent authentic. Each individual was thoroughly interviewed, allowing the transcripts to be written and edited through their voices, from their vantage points. The intention was to provide a setting of intimate discussion—a fortunate encounter with a stranger over coffee to which s/he decides to bless you with a story near and dear to the heart. These stories are real. They are raw. They are vulnerable. Each one is beyond humbling, offering an unparalleled gratitude for the blessings that we have, and a reminder of how miniscule our daily troubles tend to be.

This book was created to provide guidance, hopefully bridging the gap between what has led each of us, how our paths were discovered, as well as what helped us to maintain focus along those paths. It was created to shed some light on the periodic darkness that can overcome us if we're not careful. And created for those who hunger for something, but aren't quite sure what that something is, needing a little extra nudge to continue their pursuits.

We all crave progress, but how do we achieve it? Additionally, what progress are we making if we are not sharing and appreciating each other's moments? And not just the joyous ones where the pieces fall together, but the arduous moments as well—those where we feel powerless toward the pieces themselves.

> **"What do we live for, if it is not to make life less difficult for each other?"**
> ~George Eliot

As for my story, which sparked this inquisitive journey, and the results that unfolded during subsequent years—I'll let the details speak for themselves ....

# CHAPTER 2

## My Story ~ Making the Choice

*"I will love the light for it shows me the way,
yet I will endure the darkness for it shows me the stars."*
~Og Mandino

*I* was slowly crumbling, falling apart on the hospital's cold bathroom floor, struggling to regain my composure to discuss the test results. My soon-to-be father-in-law, one of the hospital's surgeons, met my sister and me in the lobby. He had graciously offered to walk us through what we were viewing on the glowing MRI image.

My family and I had just barely made it home from a treacherous vacation in the Dominican Republic—and believe me, I never thought I'd place the words "vacation," "Dominican Republic," and "treacherous" together in the same sentence. However, after witnessing Dad's belligerent, out-of-character outbursts, in addition to his chronic headaches and near-falls to the ground, treacherous it was. Something was very wrong, and whatever that was, it wasn't an ordinary illness.

And so we were back in Michigan, hearing the details behind our dreaded nightmare. A shotgun sounded, signaling the start to an unforeseen race, as we desperately struggled to make out the finish line.

## Allow Me to Introduce You

From June 1968 to April 1970, my father, Dr. Daniel C. Gramzow, served as an SP5 Sergeant Fifth Class in Preventive Medicine during the Vietnam War. After he returned to the States, he married my mother, raised four daughters, and continued his career as a chiropractor in Mt. Clemens, Michigan. He was hard-working, honest, forgiving, and his heart was as big as they come. His lovable qualities and talents were endless, including his random whistling bouts, his mouth-watering pasta with prosciutto and asparagus, and his tendency to hide Oreos in a bowl of broken graham crackers with the hope of avoiding an "eating healthy" lecture from one of his girls.

Dad's positive influence was always within reach. My sisters and I would pile in our van after an event, eager to discuss what had taken place. "Did you see that? I can't believe he did that!" one of us would spout.

As the banter continued, Dad drove silently. He wouldn't utter a word, and yet, by not engaging in the conversation, he was sending the loudest message possible: What is the point of this conversation? Is it positive? No? Then let's talk about something else.

Dad fully invested himself in his office—mind and body—five long days each week. From time to time, a patient would humbly admit that he could no longer afford Dad's care. Upon due-diligent consideration, Dad would do his best to provide care for the person in need, despite the appropriate payment plan. Unexpected kindness—a true gift. Not to mention, yet another lesson Dad's vigilant daughters absorbed like sponges.

\* \* \*

That agonizing day, January 10, 2007, my father was diagnosed with brain cancer—Glioblastoma Multiforme (GBM)—classified by the National Brain Tumor Society as the "deadliest of malignant primary brain tumors in adults."[1] My sister and I stared in disbelief at the MRI, revealing the detestable mass overtaking a quarter of our father's brain, quickly spreading to the remaining quadrants. It's horrifically surreal, and yet astonishing how much life can change in twenty-four hours. Even in a week. Just two weeks earlier we were celebrating Dad's birthday on Christmas Day. Now we were struggling to get him to his next one.

> **"Life is not what I thought it was twenty-four hours ago ...
> and I'm not who I thought I was twenty-four hours ago.
> Still I'm singing, 'Spirit, take me up in arms with You.'"**
> ~Switchfoot

Revelations

At that stage in my life, most of my time was devoted to research. It was not only innate within me, but the core of my educational studies. I investigated everything, wanting to know the "why" behind any unknown, or at least the variables that played a role in supporting or opposing a concept.

I needed to determine what had caused my dad's illness. What could have possibly played a part in such an extreme and sudden diagnosis besides the typical statistical odds of acquiring cancer? This didn't appear to be just *any* cancer. A missing puzzle piece had to exist. Knowing wouldn't necessarily change Dad's prognosis, but when you're up against an elusive ghost, anything tangible can provide even the slightest bit of clarity as to what you're fighting and why. Research and statistics are not the end-all be-all. However, that doesn't mean we shouldn't arm ourselves with knowledge at every opportunity.

I sat on the floor in the living room of my parents' house, trusty laptop in hand, digging into any and all factors within Dad's life that

---

[1] "Tumor Types." *National Brain Tumor Society.* Web. 13 January 2013.

could have imprinted his road, leading him to this location. I shouted possibilities to my mom in the kitchen, "Maybe it was this ... maybe it was that .... Here are the odds that this may have played a part ...."

Mom inched around the corner and peered at me through the entryway. With slight hesitation, she asked, "Alicia, have you ever heard of Agent Orange?"

I was about to be enlightened. The alleged assumption exists that my father's malignancy was a direct result of exposure to Agent Orange, a defoliant (containing small amounts of dioxin) that the U.S. armed forces used for herbicidal warfare during the Vietnam War[2].

My mind and heart raced. "Mom ... you have *got* to be kidding me."

Dad had known; he had known that this could one day be in his deck of cards.

\* \* \*

You can imagine the tidal wave of emotions that ensued. To watch Dad's endless symptoms as the tumor progressed was absolutely agonizing: excruciating headaches, loss of balance, and eventually the use of his limbs and speech. Not to mention behavioral anomalies emerging like a curve ball when we least expected it. The result of putting pressure on particular locations within the brain is astounding and yet haunting. My father, the man I'd known all my life, occasionally possessed the characteristics of a complete stranger.

I quickly determined I would not attribute these atypical tendencies to him. So, from that day forward, I started my list—a list of moments with Dad. I wanted to make sure I could recall everything, just in case. Every day I'd add an item. I may not have been able to control "the plan" for Dad's life, or even mine for that matter, but I'd document it as best I could. No one could take that away from me.

---

[2] "Agent Orange and Cancer." American Cancer Society, Inc. Web. 14 October 2013.

## Stepping into the Arena

Devastation. Anger. Fear. Frustration. These are only a handful of the emotions that left us feeling weak and defenseless. The most obvious target to cast our slew of emotions toward was the government. Whether these feelings (or the logic behind them) were right or wrong, it really didn't matter. We needed an outlet. Unfortunately, not verbalizing our perspectives at that time was rather impossible. In our minds, our father sacrificed his life in Vietnam, only to eventually be killed—not by the hand of the enemy but allegedly by a poison disseminated by those who were responsible for protecting him. Anger is understandable. Justice is unattainable. But most importantly, peace is imperative, no matter what the cause or the outcome.

Even in his lowest moments, our father did not share these feelings. Not a drop of regret, resentment, or anger leaked from his lips.

"But Dad, aren't you angry?" my sister asked.

"I helped a lot of people. That's what matters," he replied.

Dad knew a divine plan existed. I suppose that's always the hardest thing to swallow: No matter how well we map out our lives, there's always a better plan, by *Someone* smarter.

> **"'For I know the plans I have for you,' says the Lord. 'They are plans for good and not for disaster, to give you a future and a hope.'"**
> *Jeremiah 29:11*
> *(NLT)*

\* \* \*

Initially, the neurosurgeon recommended attempting to remove the tumor through surgery. The hospital staff wheeled Dad in his bed to receive an MRI, the first of many preoperative procedures.

"Where's Dad?" I asked after rushing to his hospital room.

"You just missed him, Alicia. They took him to get his MRI. If you hurry you may be able to catch him, though!" Mom said.

I sprinted down the white, sterile halls toward the radiology department. I knew the hospital very well, having worked in the laboratory for years. I had to give Dad one last hug from his baby girl before surgery. I needed him to feel my belief in him, if only through the strength in my arms.

As I turned the last corner, I spotted Dad's bed disappearing into the examination room.

"Dad! Wait!" I shouted.

My arms quickly wrapped around him as I attempted to barricade my tears. Forcing myself to let go, I stared directly into his heavy blue eyes.

"Fight like hell, Dad," I said.

"You know I will," he replied.

I did know. And that was enough.

Eight nauseating hours later, the neurosurgeon entered the anxiety-cloaked waiting room. Exhaustion and relief painted his face as we all screamed with joy. Dad had made it! Not only had he survived the surgery, but the miraculous presumption was made that every last fragment of the tumor had been removed.

As I curbed my urge to tackle the doctor in a mammoth bear-hug, I caught a subtle but distinct look in his eye. The hint of restraint. This wasn't over—far from it. While deep down we knew he was right, then and there we rejoiced. Dad was still with us! Round one of the battle had been won. We were far from being out of the woods, but at least the trees had temporarily cleared enough for us to breathe again.

The next day, my mother, my aunt, and I walked into Dad's trauma unit room. Our excitement to visit our victorious patient overflowed, dwarfing any suggested caution as to what we were about to witness. After removing a tumor of massive dimensions, occupying a large portion of space in the brain, a significant amount of spatial shift was in store. Matter was readjusting and repositioning itself within Dad's brain. His body furiously jerked up and down uncontrollably on his bed. Disorientation and pain consumed him.

His cold eyes shot toward me, cutting like jagged shards of glass. I knew what he was telling me. Obeying his wishes, I quickly left the trauma unit.

My legs carried me as far as the parking lot before momentum ceased. My vision bounced from car to car like a pinball. *What just happened!* As I attempted to regain composure, reality gripped my shoulders. Round two was in full effect, with little time to prepare. Yet Dad moved forward like a champ, enduring chemotherapy and radiation just as the doctors prescribed.

## Forced Reality

Throughout my childhood, moments existed when I swore Dad knew everything. He would humbly retain and share knowledge at the request of any inquisitive mind. However, post-surgery, Dad fought for every bit of strength and brain power that he possessed pre-operation. As he and I flipped through a children's book, practicing recognition of basic objects and the pronunciation of *ball*, my anger mounted tenfold at his pain and unnecessary obstacles.

"Thank you, honey," he said as he cradled the book close to his chest.

"You're welcome, Dad," I managed to say.

My heart tore as he sincerely thanked me for a book I had never anticipated him needing. He accepted my gift as if it were a treasure—a solid step on his road to healing. No one ever wishes to see her parent in that state. I certainly didn't think I'd witness it at the age of twenty-six. Life had come full circle, much too soon.

\* \* \*

As every weekend with Dad came to an end in Michigan, I headed back to Cincinnati for school. Walking out that door was excruciating. The inevitable tug-of-war never failed to occur: a long drive, class, and my internship, versus Dad's hand reinforcing his grip with mine as I reluctantly attempted to pull away.

at a minimum. But that was okay. The fabulous Italian that she is, I assure you, her meat sauce was worth enduring the accompaniment of health-conscious noodles. During the entire four-and-a-half hour drive home from college, at the end of a long week filled with nothing but frozen meals and Kraft macaroni and cheese, I fantasized about a home-cooked meal.

The cancer continued to attack Dad's body, diminishing the use of his physical capabilities. Despite that, Mom, Dad, and I sat at the dining room table, ready to devour our savory treat. Dad's hand crept toward his fork, eager to twirl those noodles. But his muscles fought him—not just in twirling, but gripping the utensil all-together. With a momentary grimace, he deliberately dropped his fork and dove in, using only his hands as tools. Tears filled our eyes as Dad grabbed his noodles with whatever clutching capabilities still remained, gratefully bringing the warm sustenance to his lips.

Following Dad's lead, I slid my fork back onto the table. After my first handful, the image in my peripheral vision became unavoidable.

Dad's eyes focused from beneath his silver framed glasses onto my sauce-splattered hands. Chewing halted as his grimace reappeared. In an utterly silent room, his words were loud and clear: "Honey, you're crazy! I love you, but pick up that dang fork. No one should choose to live like this."

Message received. I begrudgingly wiped off my fingers and reached for my fork, hating that he wanted to ride this coaster alone, but loving him even more because he wasn't afraid to do it.

* * *

Do I believe that our father honestly thought he'd overcome the cancer? No. Do I think he fought tremendously hard for the sake of his family alone? Yes. Even among his most difficult and final days, Dad never ceased making his girls feel loved, beautiful, and appreciated.

## He Had Somewhere Else to Be

On November 13, 2007, Dad passed away at the age of sixty-three, only two weeks before Ryan's and my wedding day. Even after the pain he endured, and the years robbed from him with his wife, children, and someday grandchildren, he still believed being a veteran was worth it, possessing nothing but pride in his service. *He* was our miracle, and we were his. In the end, all of our moments, good and bad, are worth the pain of the loss. His life on earth couldn't last forever no matter how badly we wanted it to, but he could certainly live on in each of us.

### Now what?

After my father's death, I didn't know how to move forward. Not just how to, but honestly, why *should* I? What was the point? While this may seem dramatic, in the moment this is an extremely sincere void that needs to be experienced in order to be fully understood. Death is of course a part of life, but the early, excruciating death of a man who was the glue of our family and who had blessed more lives than many can fathom—*that* was devastating. In my mind, it couldn't be justified.

I eventually realized that every day was a *choice*: a choice to get out of bed; a choice to decide to take one minute, one hour, one day at a time; a choice to brighten my surroundings, for myself, and for those whom I love; a choice to enjoy life, despite any guilt, fear, or void that may still remain; a choice to trust God fully, knowing he holds the entire puzzle in his hands, while I can only see a handful of the pieces.

> **"Our behavior is a function of our decisions, not our conditions."**
> ~Stephen R. Covey

Though I realized this, I could never have too many reminders as to how and why to make that choice. Life had blindsided me, and in turn, I wanted nothing to do with it. From then on, I was on a journey to figure out how to not only find joy again, but how to maintain it. One fundamental passion pushing me onward is the book that you hold in your hands—what began as an idea of how to help others overcome life's challenges and/or be inspired by another's dedication toward healing and triumph.

My father did not suffer or die in vain. In fact, this book was created in a sense *because* he lived. We all ponder why life's circumstances play out as they have. What good could possibly come from undeserved, indescribable pain and hardship? It's never easy, that's for sure. However, sometimes if we're lucky, what once was dark and empty can turn into a tiny, significant seed.

> **"In most solemn truth I tell you that unless the grain of wheat falls into the ground and dies, it remains what it was—a single grain; but that if it dies, it yields a rich harvest."**
> *John 12:24*
> *(WNT)*

## Reflection Questions

1. One of the hardest aspects of having an illness is the "waiting game." This can encompass waiting on test results, a pending prognosis, and the determination of likely "causes." Do you think Alicia discovering the alleged "why" behind her father's cancer made his diagnosis easier to swallow? Would you have wanted to know?

2. Alicia admitted her regret in not spending more time with her father, despite her responsibilities and obligations. What would you do in a similar situation? Do you think a different decision would have made a significant difference?

3. Is there a difficult moment in your past or present, which upon re-evaluation, may resemble a seed for growth?

# CHAPTER 3

## Ben's Story ~ A Collision of Miracles

*"I would rather walk with God in the dark*
*than go alone in the light."*
*~Mary Gardiner Brainard*

he clock struck 6:50 a.m. as I ran an early-morning errand for work. My Honda Accord trekked along Altamont Road, a two-lane street, at about thirty miles an hour in a little town called Tracy City. Drizzle fell, making the combination of rain and oil from the road a bit dangerous. I rounded a slight turn as an oncoming car flashed from the corner of my eye. Only about fifty feet away, the 280 Z sports car was already sideways and flying toward me at rapid speed. *Oh Lord, we're gonna hit!* I couldn't do anything to stop it. The side of the sports car hit my vehicle head-on.

\* \* \*

What a great week it had been! I had been working with a non-profit Christian ministry called Mountain T.O.P. (Tennessee Outreach Project)[3] in Southeast Tennessee, repairing homes for needy families. On the last day of camp, August 9, 1991, a great deal of work remained, making it necessary for me to run an errand early that morning. A carved wooden cross, made by a close friend of mine,

---

[3] Mountain T.O.P: http://www.mountain-top.org/

dangled from my rear-view mirror, providing a constant reminder of my ultimate safety. But, the accident was like a lightning bolt that I could not prevent. There was no walking away from this one.

The police report stated that the twenty-seven-year-old driver was traveling at a very high speed (approximately fifty to fifty-five miles per hour) on the wrong side of the road. Hearing what could only be compared to dynamite exploding, a nearby home-owner ran toward the crash. The powerful impact not only knocked me out instantly, but also propelled my toolbox from the trunk straight through the back seat.

Soon the local rescue squad arrived. The front of my car was non-existent. The entire engine, dashboard, and steering column pinned my chest and legs against the seat. The initial responder inspected my body, finally making his announcement.

"I can't find a pulse, guys."

Meanwhile, team members worked to remove the other driver from the wreckage.

A rescue worker preparing to remove my body shouted in panic, "Guys, we've got a pulse! We've gotta get him out of there!"

Consciousness came and went. When I did come to, the thundering roar from the Jaws of Life® rang in my ears. Initially, I experienced only a little pain … and then it hit. My head exploded in a relentless throb, as if it had been cracked open with a baseball bat.

"Hold on! We're going to get you out of there, just hold on!"

A white sheet fell over my body. *They think I'm dead … they think I'm dead!* But the Jaws of Life® continued to roar as it fought to pull the steering column off my legs and chest.

"Guys, we're losing him! We're losing him—we've gotta hurry! Hold on, pal, we're getting you out."

With determination, the squad crawled through the shattered back window and sides of the car. I had been storing two bags of insulation in the front seat, now shredded and scattered throughout the entire inside. But this didn't slow them down—inch-by-inch they forced their way toward me. Approximately an hour later, my body was finally pulled from the vehicle and placed gently on the backboard. *Well, my back's broken. I know my back is broken.*

\* \* \*

I was taken to Emerald Hodgson Hospital in Sewanee, TN, while Life Flight was contacted to transport me to Murfreesboro\*, TN. Two physicians talked to me, making simple requests. "I need you to squeeze my finger for me, Ben\*. *Squeeze. Finger,*" they clearly said. Yet my hand refused to respond.

Life Flight arrived. The deafening noise of the engine and propeller pierced my already pounding skull, while its swooping blades gushed wind over my body. Were they going to strap me to the outside of the helicopter? Clearly I had watched one too many episodes of *MASH.*

"Ahhhhhh!" I screamed in agony, while calling the flight-nurse every name in the book—a clear indication of my serious head injury.

In the meantime, my folks had been contacted. "Your son has been in a very serious auto accident. He has massive head, chest, and leg injuries and his condition is extremely critical. Life Flight Helicopter is transporting Ben to Raintree Medical Center\* in Murfreesboro. Y'all need to start moving down here."

My parents lived in Nashville, about forty minutes northwest. Worry and panic grew as each mile fell behind them.

Life in Critical Care

After being unconscious for several hours, my body slowly returned to life as the reality of the situation hit. My stomach was on fire! The hospital staff had observed a giant bruise across my chest and rib cage, prompting them to run an Arteriogram (one in an endless stream of tests) to determine if I had torn my aorta as a result of the immense impact. The properties in the dye from the Arteriogram made their way through my system, leaving a sensation as if I were burning from the inside out! In a state such as mine, hospital staff generally refrains from administering sedating pain medication to prevent the patient from losing consciousness, also allowing the ability to monitor mental status closely. So unfortunately, my pain had to be confronted head on. Everyone kept telling me how fortunate I was, but I struggled to see how that was true.

My parents rushed to my side in the emergency room, tears flooding their eyes. I couldn't help but join them. Mom was afraid to even touch me. And yet, curiosity was killing her. Her hand crept toward my mouth.

"Yep, he still has his teeth," she said to my dad with a sigh of relief.

Dad was an attorney, so I knew he and my mother had been mulling over everything that could have caused the crash during their drive. They knew I was a safe driver. I would never let drugs or alcohol enter the picture.

That first night, approximately twelve beds formed a u-shape around the Trauma ICU. Yet ironically, the staff placed Russell*, the man who hit me, in the bed directly next to mine. Both of Russell's legs/hips were crushed in the crash. He was very weak, having lost a lot of blood. But thankfully, our families weren't hostile. Causing a scene would only make the situation worse.

"Ben, you do not have anything to worry about," I was assured.

\* \* \*

I was connected to various machines. My right ankle was shattered, my right knee cap was cracked, and three toes on my left foot were broken. I had numerous broken ribs, two cracked orbital bones, and a broken nose. Both of my lungs were deflated, demanding me to struggle for every breath. A blood clot was also forming in my skull, symptomatically manifesting in blurry vision. I had two large black eyes and my neck, head, chest, and legs were extremely bruised and swollen.

I'm sure I was unrecognizable. Several visitors passed out in front of me. Four visitation periods were permitted during the day in the

Trauma ICU. The first was at 4:30 in the morning. My parents were always there, waiting to enter my room. Each minute crawled by on the clock above the main nurse's station as I awaited someone familiar.

\* \* \*

The first seven or eight days were extremely grueling. I was lucid enough to understand what was going on around me. An agonizing sensation existed in my neck, as if my jaw had been completely disconnected. I tried to communicate to the hospital staff that my neck was broken, but was repeatedly told that the pain was a result of whiplash. They placed me in a soft neck collar to limit movement, provide support, and hopefully, alleviate pain. Due to my extensive head injury, Liquid Tylenol was the only medication I was allowed, having to be administered through a feeding tube guided into my nose. I begged for a more potent pain medicine, desperately needing them to understand! I needed some type of relief, no matter how small. But my next request surprised even me:

"Oh my gosh, *please* let me go. Just let me go…" I pleaded over and over, directed not only to the staff, but to God Himself.

\* \* \*

The majority of the Raintree Trauma team were wonderful. The day-shift staff acted responsibly. However, I dreaded the night-shift hours. Bright lights streamed over me 24/7, in addition to the constant noise. I grabbed a towel and placed it over my head, desperate for some sleep. But just as quickly as the light dimmed, its intensity returned. *What happened to my towel?* I grasped aimlessly for its familiar texture.

"I'll break your g!&%damn arm off if you don't stop," the Respiratory Therapist said as he began the process of suctioning fluid from my lungs.

That was only the beginning. Under the impression that I was unconscious, the night-shift technicians would describe their recent

three days. Due to the tracheostomy, I was extremely weak and unable to verbally communicate.

"Okay, Ben, we're going to ask you some questions and we need you to respond. We need you to blink your response. One blink will mean 'yes' and two blinks will mean 'no.' Do you understand?" the doctor asked.

*I blinked.*

"Good. We're now going to give you some simple math questions and we want you to do them for us. What is two plus one?"

*I blinked three times.*

"What is five minus four?"

*Again, I did the equation.*

"Wow … somebody get his family."

The rest of the day I repeatedly heard staff members uttering, "I don't believe it. I just *don't* believe it."

I was very weak but thrilled to finally be sedated for the first time—what a great gift to awaken to! My right leg, having significant damage, still awaited an operation. I anticipated them needing to amputate it above the ankle, yet I had no idea what was in store.

Throughout this commotion, I couldn't let go of what had just happened to me. It was incredible! But I couldn't share it … at least not for a while. It had to be with the right person. In the meantime, I was curious how much the initial experience matched my surroundings. When I first glided away from my hospital room, I lowered onto a patch of grass next to a parking lot. Was that possible? I had to find out.

"What floor are we on?" I jotted down on a piece of paper, handing it to the nurse.

"We're on the fourth floor," she replied.

"What's on the other side of this wall?" I wrote.

"A parking lot."

My heart beat faster.

About a month later, the associate pastor from my church in Nashville came to visit. I still couldn't speak at the time but was prepared, having my encounter thoughtfully written out on paper, waiting to be shared.

As he read, his eyebrows lifted increasingly with each sentence, while his forehead reduced to a compressed stream of creases. "Wow. Wow. Wow," he repeated.

I also shared my story with a Christian friend. She's a very compassionate woman, serving others as a hospice nurse in Nashville.

"Ben, it was the drugs," she stated matter-of-factly.

"Yep, it could have been," I replied, pausing before I continued. "However, you are also the one that told me you only visit patients if you thought they were going to die."

"Yes. But I knew if I didn't come to see you, you would be disappointed in me," she teased.

I laughed along with her, but I knew … she had feared this might be the end.

## Humpty Dumpty

Thousands of friends and strangers alike had been praying for me to survive. My church in Nashville, Mountain T.O.P., a number of churches in the Mountain T.O.P community, and those connected through Young Life[4] ministries had all been spreading the word of my condition. Even the children had been praying for me, which impacted me greatly. Children see straight through to the heart of the matter, whispering directly into God's ears.

And such an overwhelming number of cards! My mom was a dietitian at a parochial school, collecting more than 500 get-well cards from students, grades kindergarten through eighth. A card from a third grader stands out in my mind, being one of at least two or three letters from this child alone. It read, "I'm really getting tired of praying for you. Please get better." Sealed with a sad face.

I laughed at his words in shock. Nothing but honesty—and thank God for that!

---

[4] Young Life: https://www.younglife.org

**"Truly, I say to you, unless you turn and become like children,**
**you will never enter the kingdom of heaven. Whoever humbles**
**himself like this child is the greatest in the kingdom of heaven."**
Matthew 18:3-4
(ESV)

\* \* \*

Tracheostomy (or trach) care was performed on a regular basis to remove fluids directly from my lungs, leaving me extremely weak. Again, most patients are unconscious during this process, unlike me. I vomitted almost every time. Still being unable to swallow, I had to receive all liquids through my nose tube, making the thirst factor still a major problem. Though the pain medication helped greatly, I continued to communicate through scribbled words:

"My jaw literally feels disconnected from my neck bone."

It *couldn't* have been my imagination.

Thirteen days after my accident, the orthopedist said, "Ben, you're stabilized enough now for us to perform surgery on your right leg and ankle. We have to do it before the bone sets."

The surgery was scheduled for the following day. I awoke afterward wanting to die all over again. I peered down at my legs, both wrapped in casts. The right leg was considerably worse, constantly having ice applied and bandages replaced. Though my pain medication had been increased, the searing sensation of fire had returned. I knew I was going to lose this leg. However, at that time, I didn't care. I was Humpty Dumpty being put back together again.

\* \* \*

I remained in the Trauma ICU for a total of three weeks. The doctors still didn't understand why I was unable to swallow, continuing to run a consistent 102/103 temperature. One evening, three young patients rolled into the unit, each suffering gunshot wounds to the head. Shortly after their arrival, the coroner came to pronounce each of them dead, slowly rolling them out. *When would the coroner be coming over to my bed?*

My high fever remained constant as I was moved from the Trauma ICU to Step-Down Critical Care during my final week at Raintree. I had a private room, but sleep was still impossible. Yet, hope rose as the nurse handed me a cup of apple juice poured over crushed ice. Slowly, the soothing liquid made its way down my throat. I didn't want it to stop! Eight cups later I finally called it quits, only to vomit up every drop a few hours later. Again, my spirit was broken.

Questions constantly swam through my mind. I never asked, "Why me?" I suppose I knew that question would remain unanswered. But "How am I going to handle this financially?" was a gaping-hole question, always in the back of my head. I would not only have immense health-care bills in the future to maintain my condition, whatever that may be, but also I'd have to pay one hundred percent of my current hospital bills ... which had only just begun to accrue. Unbeknownst to me, my dad and a family friend had carefully reviewed my insurance policies during the first few days after the accident. I had car insurance, health insurance, a separate hospital-income policy, and a worker's compensation policy.

"Do *not* worry about that, Ben. You do not need to worry," my family and friends would repeat.

But that was easier said than done. I did not want anyone else to support me. I wanted to take care of myself.

\* \* \*

Even though frequently lost in intense pain, I was fully aware of the behind-the-scenes planning. Transportation to get me back to Nashville was a priority. A large process is involved when transporting patients with severe injuries. Eager to help, I suggested using a friend's ambulance service. With the help of my family, we got everything situated for me to travel back home to Nashville's Cumberview Park Hospital\*.

No one knew how I was going to respond to what was about to happen. This was new territory for everyone involved.

The staff shaved the sides of my head, injecting a needle of Novocain into my skull slightly above each ear. Next, the neuro-team quickly drilled screws into both sides of my skull. I literally went *out of my mind!* My deep, roaring screams could not be controlled, piercing the ears surrounding me. It truly was worse than anything I had ever imagined. Each of my family members broke down in tears, racing from the room in horror. Their exit gave me a bit of relief—the absolute worst thing in the world to experience was seeing my mother cry. It tore me up, perhaps as much as any medical procedure ever could.

The traction device was then attached as accurately and swiftly as possible. It was a huge, painfully magnificent system. I was placed in a special bed, enabling the precise position of the device. The Gardner-Wells Tongs, shaped like a half-moon, extended above the top portion of my head, and were held in place by two screws, each above my right and left ear. Attached to the tongs, a cervical-traction pulley system stretched out directly behind me from the top of my skull, held in place by thirty-five pounds of weights dangling beneath.[5] I remained flat on my back, only able to look directly at the ceiling for eight days.

"Due to the traction device, we think your skull is going to move into its correct location. If it does, you're going to hear a 'pop,'" the neurosurgeon told me.

"Is it going to hurt?" I asked.

"You're definitely going to feel it. But let us know *immediately.* Your skull will be very unstable, requiring immediate surgery. But this device will bring you great relief, Ben."

I wanted to trust him about that, but you can imagine how I'd be nervous. Yet the doctor was right. My pain was reduced incredibly by this contraption that brought fear to the average eye.

---

[5] Thompson, Stephen R. and Dan A. Zlotolow. *Handbook of Splinting and Casting: Mobile Medicine Series.* Philadelphia: Mosby, Inc., 2012. Print.

## Strength in Numbers

Lots of friends and family were with me day in and day out. A few of the Cumberview Park Hospital staff even took the time to visit me at Baptist. Just knowing I wasn't alone got me through. Though I had few expectations, I knew it could be hard knowing the "right" thing to say when visiting a hospital patient. Visitors provided supportive comments, unaware of what those before them had shared. Ironically (or maybe not), over and over again, a specific verse in scripture was given to me. God didn't want me to forget this, and continuously ensured each word:

> **"And the peace of God, which surpasses all understanding,**
> **will guard your hearts and minds through Christ Jesus."**
> *Philippians 4:7*
> *(NKJV)*

Prayers were sent upward by the thousands. When picturing an hourglass, the two bulbs that contain the sand are linked by a connecting tube in order to allow the sand to pass through, keeping track of time. Right there, in the center of that connecting tube—that was me—that's where I was. All of those sands were prayers. They couldn't pass without touching me. I could literally *feel* the support—the faithful words, the driven hearts, the bottomless hope. I knew that's how I had made it this far … and a little valium didn't hurt either.

## Provoked Smiles

During my eight days of traction, things were attached to many areas of my body—tubes here, patches connected to wires there. Every part of me was constantly monitored. But as long as I didn't laugh I was comfortable. The phone was within reach and the TV was elevated and at an angle, allowing me to see the screen without trouble.

The staff was amazing, always doing their best to accommodate me. My nurses were special. They really "got" me. In a lot of ways, I wasn't their typical patient. Sadly, many who came into this unit never left alive. But I was fairly lucid. Though I'm sure there wasn't *always* time for my jokes, they took them awfully well. Occasionally, I'd yank every cord within reach, disconnecting them from my body, instantly sounding alarms. Before the nurses had a chance to reach me, I'd reattach each of them in their appropriate places, extinguishing the alarms as if nothing had happened.

"What'd you do, Ben? We know you did *something*, but we don't know what!"

Despite the pain it would cause, I couldn't help but laugh hysterically.

\* \* \*

My sister worked in the cosmetics department at Dillard's. I quickly dialed her number with a specific favor in mind.

"Do you think you could bring in as many free high-end perfume samples as possible?" I asked.

On her next visit, she arrived with about two-hundred bottles in tow. I eagerly called all the nurses into my room.

"What do you want, Ben? We're busy."

"I've got something for you," I said with a grin.

Both of my legs were still in casts, covered by a bed sheet. I tipped the Dillard's bag, causing the surplus of perfume to tumble across the sheet. Their faces lit up while they shrieked with excitement. Arms swarmed every which way, grabbing for as many bottles as their hands could hold. I'd do anything to see those smiles.

## The Day Was Near

Unfortunately, the traction device was unable to realign my skull as the doctors had hoped. Due to this, my head would forever remain fused, slightly twisted and tilted to the right. Major surgery was approaching, and each day my concern grew considerably.

My neurosurgeon explained that he was going to re-attach the skull to the vertebrae. "I just want you to prepare yourself, Ben. This will be a very long and difficult surgery."

The day came. October 15, 1991. I knew there was a good chance I might be paralyzed, or perhaps not even survive the surgery. But again, somehow the Lord calmed any fear or anxiety within me. I could be in heaven in only a few hours.

Sandy, a nurse to whom I had become close, came to visit me just prior to the surgery. "Ben, I want to take you down to the operating room with the team."

"I'd appreciate that, Sandy. But also, would you mind praying for me—you and your family?" I had never approached that subject with her before, but something told me I could.

"*Absolutely*," she responded.

I asked Dr. Landrove to wheel me down to the operating room as well. The more friendly faces surrounding me, the better. As they pushed my massive bed (still supporting the traction device) toward the operating room, I watched with a sick stomach as the neuro-nurses—some of the toughest nurses in the business—had tears glossing over their eyes.

Typical protocol before having any major surgery includes placing a tube down the patient's throat to allow breathing (normally only taking less than a minute). However, given the precarious nature of my neck, my jaw had to be lifted in order to run the tube downward. Several failed attempts and my consistent gagging required a Plan B.

"Okay, we're going to have to scope it down," the anesthesiologist said.

I could sense the apprehension from the team. Administering an additional sedative to put me under was now necessary to move forward.

Something told me: After everything I had experienced and all the pain already endured, even *I* wasn't prepared for what was ahead of me. Dr. Landrove and Nurse Patty (whom I referred to as my angel) held each of my hands firmly as shots were injected into my neck.

*Okay Lord. This is it. I am not afraid of dying. I'm ready for heaven. I don't want to hurt my family and friends ... but, I'm ready.* I drifted into unconsciousness, leaving my life in the team's hands.

\* \* \*

At 10:00 p.m. that evening, approximately seven hours later, I returned to consciousness with the immediate sensation of bright lights beaming into my eyes. Was I in heaven? No, the pain was too intense. I was in the recovery room. I couldn't move or speak due to the various tubes running into my mouth and covering my skin. Recalling the possibility of paralysis, I attempted to kick each of my legs. The sheets draped over me were moving! Thank You, Lord!

The next attempt was to move my arms. Nothing. No movement whatsoever. I became frantic, struggling to verify the use of any possible arm muscle. *Nothing* was happening!

A nurse ran over declaring, "Calm down, Ben. Calm down. You're strapped down."

Again, thank You God!

\* \* \*

During surgery, my neck was fused from the skull to the first, second, and third vertebra using a nine inch titanium horse-shoe-shaped rod. Cartilage had also been removed from all three vertebrae and replaced with bone removed from my hip. Yet, my difficult days were far from behind me. I remained in the Neuro-ICU for eighteen days while numerous tests were performed.

But after everything ... riding this roller coaster of pain, more than three months of care at four different hospitals, and more unanswered questions than I could count, my physicians were able to provide an answer to the one question that had haunted me since day one: I would be able to live a relatively normal life. A true miracle.

## Rays of Sunshine

I stayed at Baptist one more month for intensive rehab. On Halloween, some friends brought in their five kids and their neighbor's three children to surprise me in their costumes. Those eight giggling children entered my hospital room, excited to see my face as I observed their disguises. My smile could not be contained! After witnessing how thrilled the nurses were to see our trick-or-treaters, I had an idea.

"Hey guys," I said in a whisper, "let's go for a rooooll." The Neuro-ICU was strict on visitors, but maybe just this once they'd make an exception.

I hadn't been up there in a while, so I couldn't wait to show off my new state of movement, even if I was only wheelchair bound. I raised my hand and punched the bell, ringing the head desk.

Sandy approached my gang. "Oh my gosh! Hold on just one second," she exclaimed with joy as she took off to round up the other nurses and able patients.

In Neuro, seldom do many of the patients return to their normal lives. Most are unconscious. For those who weren't, today was special. They obviously couldn't be a part of Halloween, so we would bring Halloween to them. Mounds of food, candy, and smiles were eager to be pulled from the cobwebs. The kids dove into the little pumpkins and M&Ms, oblivious to the huge ray of sunshine that they had managed to pull through the clouds.

* * *

The staff at Baptist Hospital became like family. Dr. Landrove stopped by every morning around 7:00 to deliver my newspaper, always returning at the end of the day to see how I was holding up. Because of their help and guidance, I could walk without any support after only an additional three to four months.

> **"I walk slowly, but I never walk backward."**
> ~Abraham Lincoln

## Listening for Answers

I didn't always know what lay on the road ahead of me. One day could be completely different from the next. But despite that, I was able to drive six to eight months after my rehabilitation began. I strived to exercise on a regular basis, either swimming or riding a stationary bicycle. Thankfully, my incredible pain pump (buried beneath my skin) helped me deal with the day-to-day aches. The cartridge (a little bigger than a hockey puck) holds approximately four months of pain medication. This medication, an extremely strong muscle relaxer, runs up and down my spine. My daily doses are timed and controlled by a computer micro-chip, through a port on the left side of my body. The dose then runs through a catheter to the fluid around the spinal cord. You would never even know it was there.

But despite my progress, I was still angry—angry at the guy who hit me. No question about it. Because of his error in judgment, so many capabilities had been taken from me. I wasn't going to be able to snow ski, water ski, take a long run in the park, or play basketball as I used to. I was very hurt. Very disappointed.

I wasn't angry at God—I just didn't understand. I don't understand a lot of things about God, and I've accepted that I may never fully understand while on this earth. But sometimes, if we patiently listen closely to Him, we can find answers. Sometimes He tells us through our loved ones. Sometimes we have to let go of our pride and accept what we don't want to hear. I never thought such an extreme accident would happen to me. But it did. I couldn't change that. So, I needed to find a way to move past it. I needed to listen.

Trials

After I was released from the hospital, I *had* to investigate my options. I was informed that Raintree Hospital had only filmed my spine from the fifth vertebra down. Accidents do happen. However, my bills were huge, and without a doubt needed to be paid.

I decided to seek legal advice, concerned that my entire spine not being filmed meant someone had done something wrong. I consulted with several attorneys. After extensive examination, my lawyers concluded that my partial x-ray was a misdiagnosis, but would not support a claim against the hospital or the medical personnel. I didn't understand how this could be! But I couldn't hold onto a situation that wasn't going to change. Reality was upon me—I had to look into alternatives. I needed to face Russell, the driver who hit me, in court and tap into my own car and health insurance.

A definite battle was in front of me before the court would award the itemized sums accrued since the initial crash. Even more importantly, to receive an amount that would enable payment of not only my current hospital bills, but those sure to incur the rest of my life. I couldn't always contain my frustrations, no matter how hard I tried. But somehow I kept hearing the Lord say, "Don't worry. I will take care of you."

I had to trust in that as court proceedings with Russell moved forward.

> **"Do not worry about anything, but pray and ask God**
> **for everything you need, always giving thanks."**
> *Philippians 4:6*
> *(NCV)*

Upon my first meeting with my attorney, he prefaced our legal journey with, "There's always grey in a trial, Ben. It's never black and white. There's always grey."

However, in this case he was wrong. I responded with conviction, "Black. White. No question."

After seeing every bit of evidence, my attorneys agreed—it was absolutely freakish—no grey to be found.

\* \* \*

Several years passed before Russell and I met in court. Though I knew that a number of my friends and family were traveling to Altamont for the trial, I didn't realize what I would be walking into. As I entered the courtroom, the scene transported me into the movie *Hoosiers*, where a small-town team enters a gigantic stadium for the state championship basketball game, packed with more people than they could have imagined. The court system had sequestered approximately fifty-two jurors. Over the past several weeks, my attorneys prepared me for anything, covering every inch of what "could happen." Yet, I had no idea the trial would be of this magnitude. All I could do was be honest. Hopefully that would be enough.

Russell was covered under his parents' auto-insurance policy. Representation from this insurance company presented 100,000 dollars to settle their portion of the case. Panic rose within me. That amount was not going to *touch* my hospital bills! But that's all that was there. Russell had only been covered for 100,000 dollars in damages. Pursuing him further would have led to him filing for bankruptcy, eliminating debt. That wouldn't have benefited anyone. My attorney accepted the 100,000 dollars, which was placed in a special account designated toward health-care bills, although that would only be a tiny drop in a bottomless bucket.

The next step was to pursue my auto-insurance coverage. In order to reach a settlement that was fair, I had to take the stand. Again, I was in that gym, the State Championship Finals, numerous people watching. I was walking to the top of the key to shoot the free-throws that would determine the final score.

"Okay Ben, this is it," my attorney said. "We just want you to tell them your story."

The details were still quite fresh in my mind. I told them everything. At one point during my trach description, the judge issued a recess so that my poor mom could regain composure. At another point, the judge asked to cease my descriptions.

My attorney approached me after my testimony. "I really think the judge was about to get sick," he said.

I shot my free-throws, just wanting to be honest—not worrying about the score.

Though the judge ruled in my favor, my auto-insurance company appealed the judge's decision. It took several years for the case to move through the judicial system. I firmly believe it was the objective of my insurance company to wear me down through appeals, ultimately settling for a far less amount—but I refused to be intimidated.

The case finally settled. Every penny of my existing hospital bills would be paid for by the auto-insurance settlement. Though, other than the necessity of paying my health-care bills, no dollar amount would ever be worth the suffering endured and the time lost.

\* \* \*

The two auto-insurance settlements covered my past bills. However, I still had no idea how I was going to cover all of my future care, which was a significant amount. Worker's Compensation Insurance remained as an option, being that I was running an errand for work at the time of the accident. *Lord, please help pave a way* ....

I met with two attorneys from Lightgrove Insurance\*, two attorneys from the State of Tennessee attempting to mediate the case, and my two personal attorneys. The initial offer from Lightgrove was presented: "We'll offer you 3,000 dollars to settle."

I turned to my attorneys and said in disbelief, "Am I understanding this correctly? Please tell them no."

I then turned down their next insulting offer of 10,000 dollars, to which an attorney replied, "Okay, then we'll have to go before a judge."

After the hearing, the Lightgrove attorneys approached me.

"Ben, we're sorry for how we had to approach this. We are required to offer these amounts up-front," one attorney stated.

I was never looking for an actual cash settlement, but lifetime medical benefits to allow my pain and bills to be manageable. And yet another trial transpired, just as expected. As a result, and to their credit, they've supported me ever since. A gigantic weight had been lifted off my shoulders; I could finally breathe again.

> **"As long as I am breathing, in my eyes, I am just beginning."**
> ~Criss Jami

\* \* \*

Four long, frustrating years passed while completing the entire process for all the trials. I had to do it, though. I couldn't settle. My health depended on it, and I knew I could expect a future loaded with chronic pain.

## Necessary Mending

Only about four or five times have I heard the Lord speaking clearly to me, revealing something that needed to be done. One of them, without a doubt, was to get in touch with Russell. About a year had passed since our legal battle and despite what took place in the courts, the accident was in the past and needed to remain there. I wanted to see how he was doing. I wanted him to know that I was okay. That I had forgiven him. That I had moved on. So, I called up my good friend Carlyle to share my plan.

> **"The weak can never forgive. Forgiveness
> is the attribute of the strong."**
> ~Mahatma Gandhi

"Do you want me to go with you?" Carlyle asked.

"No, I need to do this on my own. If I don't come back, you'll know where I went ... but I'll be back."

I had to take those precautions for my own peace of mind.

\* \* \*

Russell lived with his parents. I drove through the center of their town, somehow knowing exactly where to turn, though I'd never visited that area in my life. My walk to the front door must have been one of the longest I've ever taken. Russell's mom pulled the door open and gazed at me.

"Hello ... do you know who I am?" I asked.

I looked very different from when she had last seen me. We never had a hostile relationship, as some would imagine. I didn't know her very well, but I knew *of* her. She was a very good woman. She had been raised by a Baptist family and truly enjoyed the simple things in life.

Her eyes welled up with tears as she managed to say, "Are you Ben?"

Her arms stretched outward, embracing me in warmth. Russell's father made his way to the door, also welcoming me with a kind hug.

We shifted into the living room and talked for about forty-five minutes, covering everything from my recovery, to how my parents were doing, to life in general. Now and then, my mind couldn't help but pull back from the conversation, thinking, *oh boy, when is this next step going to happen? How will Russell enter the picture?* I was hoping that he wasn't going to just walk in, stunned at who was sitting on his family's couch. I hoped someone would at least be able to announce that I was here.

I finally got up the nerve to ask, "Is Russell around?"

"Yeah, he's down there working on the car," his father replied.

A slight, awkward pause followed. Perhaps they were as nervous as I was. We walked outside to find Russell. His eyes widened as he caught the first glimpse of who stood before him.

I was curious to hear his version of what happened that day. The hospital staff was fearful that he would lose his legs, both having been badly crushed in the crash. Despite losing a great deal of blood during that first night, thankfully, both legs were saved.

"Do you remember the crash? What was it like in your car?" I asked.

He thought for a moment and replied, "Yeah. I was coming around the corner ...."

He continued through the details of a flashback that I'm sure he avoided as much as I did.

I never sensed any guilt, although I'm not sure I expected any.

"I forgive you, Russell. I truly just want us both to move forward and I hope you are well."

"Okay," he responded.

That was it. But I wasn't bitter. I had done what I needed to do. That was the last time I saw Russell, and probably ever will.

\* \* \*

I couldn't leave Raintree off my list. I needed closure. And I knew where to start: visit the physician who overlooked my neck injury. He had office hours available so I drove to Murfreesboro.

The waiting room was packed. As the woman behind the desk informed me of the two-hour wait, disappointment crept through me with the realization that this encounter probably wasn't going to happen.

"Can I ask your name, sir?"

"My name is Ben Kaypher*. Please tell him that I am here and that I'd just like to talk to him for a few minutes."

"Oh ... okay. Well, let's see what we can do," the woman replied, heading toward the back of the office.

I approached my two, faithful friends who came with me. "We're only going to wait fifteen minutes and then we'll leave. I really appreciate you all being here," I said.

A few minutes later, we were guided to the physician's office and asked to have a seat. During the discussion that followed, I discovered a great deal about this man whose shadow had lingered over my road to recovery. He was a Christian and came across as very kind and sincere. Though he never admitted being aware of the issues that had transpired during my stay at Raintree (but I knew with absolute certainty that he *was* aware, being that he called my family to check on me several months prior and had been informed of my condition), he did make very clear that what occurred had been the last thing in the world he would have wanted to happen.

Aside from these words, I had to leave the remaining holes in the story behind me. I would not find any benefit or satisfaction in trying to fill them. It was like talking with an old girlfriend—you just have to be nice, courteous, and keep moving. Life must go on.

> **"Yesterday is not ours to recover, but tomorrow is ours to win or lose."**
> ~Lyndon B. Johnson

\* \* \*

I continued my Murfreesboro quest, bringing food to other kind staff members at Raintree. They deserved that much. Those few kept me holding on, despite the terrifying moments. Next, we met with the Life Flight crew, including the pilot who flew me to Raintree. This team constantly visited my hospital room after the crash. Their dedication blew my mind.

Last but not least, I visited the rescue-squad who assisted the crash. This not only included meeting the county's EMTs, but also the man who led the entire local rescue squad.

"Ben, you're the only person who's ever come back to talk to us. Everyone else always finds fault," he said.

Prior to this visit, I had been informed of upsetting instances that had occurred during my rescue, where procedures should have gone more smoothly (such as the Jaws of Life® running out of gas, forcing a return to town to refuel). But that squad was there that day. They were doing the best they could in a very difficult situation. I had to trust that.

\* \* \*

I returned home and sat down at my desk. My final step was

to write my letter to Raintree's hospital administration. Raintree needed to be aware of everything I endured during my stay. I didn't do this for revenge or any conceivable justice. I only wanted to spare other patients some of what I had experienced.[6]

I made a conscious effort to compliment any staff members when possible. They didn't deserve to be overshadowed by others' less-than-professional actions. I then listed some of the atrocious behaviors that I had witnessed, suggesting investigation to prevent further occurrences. I sent the letter to the CEO, chief of staff, chairman of the board of directors, and the charge nurse toward whom I was very complimentary.

I received a return letter approximately ten days later. Every single one of my concerns had been addressed. That is, every single thing *except* my neck injury. But I knew upon writing the letter that this topic wouldn't be touched. What's important is that time had been taken to send a thoughtful response, supporting the need to voice my concerns. We've all had difficult times where we've needed the opportunity to make our voices heard. This was mine. I was not overlooked, and *that* was appreciated.

## Life Carries On

I was thirty-seven at the time of the accident. Hard to believe it's been more than twenty years. It was never my intention to degrade any institution or individual, but only share my story in a truthful and clear manner. That crash turned my world upside down. In a split second, my life was changed forever. But I can't ignore that I've made it this far because of the Lord's blessings. I am thankful to be alive. God has used my horrific experience to reach a lot of people in positive ways. And He was with me *every second* of the way.

---

[6] Described events took place approximately twenty-five years ago. Due to the great length of time between the negative incident(s) (about the hospital and its employees) and current day, it is likely few, if any, of the individuals who were there at that time still remain.

*"God is our refuge and strength, an ever-present help in trouble. Therefore we will not fear, though the earth give way and the mountains fall into the heart of the sea,"*
Psalm 46:1-2
(NIV)

Sometimes I still ask, "Why?" Not "Why did this happen," but "Why did I survive?" The truth is—I'm a very ordinary, simple person. It's just that God did something extraordinary in my life. He placed His hand on me. I don't fully understand why, and I know I will never have absolute answers. However, God blessed me despite a great deal of adversity. He continues to perform miraculous events in my life. I can't help but continue to think, Lord, You have a plan. What's happened here is just the Lord working, as only He can.

*"God specializes in using ordinary people whose limitations and weaknesses make them ideal showcases for His greatness and glory."*
*–Nancy Leigh DeMoss*

## Critical Care to Critical Certainties

I have spoken to many groups since my accident. I briefly mention my "glimpse of heaven," which always provokes further questioning. But all I know is what happened to me. This was the one and only time I ever had a vision of angels. I do not know if I was actually *in* heaven, though it was obvious that a place was being prepared for me.

This "glimpse" was a small moment in my recovery, but a very important one. I can't compare it to anyone else's spiritual experience and I definitely can't force others to believe it to be true. Yet more than ever, two certainties were embedded within me: 1) God is real; 2) in Christ, death is nothing to fear. That's what's critical.

*Names or locations have been changed to protect those involved.

## Reflection Questions

1.  Is it hard to conceive that after everything Ben fought through, the physicians pronounced that he would lead a "relatively normal life"? Ben suffered colossal injuries, but *walked* away having witnessed miracles. What does that tell us about God's power?

2.  Much debate will likely ensue regarding whether or not Ben's "glimpse of heaven" was authentic, or a result of the drugs he had been issued. Regardless of which side of the argument you fall, the true question may be, does it really matter? What did the "glimpse of heaven" experience do for Ben during this time frame? What does it say to *you*?

3.  Ben claims to be an ordinary person, experiencing extraordinary events through our Heavenly Father. Do you see power in the ordinary? How might an ordinary scenario in your life be part of a divine extraordinary plan?

4.  "Sometimes I still ask, 'Why?' Not 'Why did this happen,' but 'Why did I survive?'" This is a substantial paradigm shift: not dwelling on why a negative experience took place, but why are we able to overcome, despite massive adversity. Have you ever found triumph in a circumstance where the odds were stacked against you?

# A Collision of Miracles: Seeds of Growth

**Surround yourself with good company.**

Time and time again, Ben speaks of the family, friends, and staff that made his recovery possible. These individuals stood by him, not only in his healing, but during his court trials and his pursuit of closure. They didn't only celebrate the breakthroughs, they held his hands through the breaks themselves.

We expect to have good days, make good memories, and enjoy the time with which we are blessed. Yet, if we're not selective of the key players in our lives, how can any of those expectations ring true?

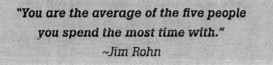

> *"You are the average of the five people you spend the most time with."*
> ~Jim Rohn

A true supporter …

> … listens to you.
> … challenges you when complacency sets in.
> … appreciates what you do and would do the same for you.
> … speaks to you with respect.
> … is honest with you, even when it hurts.
> … walks beside you on your path despite circumstances or opinions.
> … helps to lighten the load.
> … carries your dreams, even when you've set them down.
> … is a constant cheerleader.
> … supports the need for laughter.

... loves you unconditionally.
... leads you to the *Light*.

Our time is precious. Why would we give it to those who treat us with disrespect or those who do not support the values that guide us toward a positive path? Those individuals will only drag us down. Why would we want to let that happen when we're always fighting so hard to stand?

**"Whoever walks with the wise becomes wise,**
**but the companion of fools will suffer harm."**
*Proverbs 13:20*
*(ESV)*

# CHAPTER 4

## Penny's Story ~ Producing Something Beautiful

*"The wise don't expect to find life worth living; they make it that way."*
~Anonymous

My sister Terrie (my only "whole-sibling") and I were pretty close growing up, probably because we spent most of our time together while our mom was at work. We were born poor, raised poor. While Mom worked, her boyfriend Teddy would babysit. He was like the daddy we never had. Every summer weekend, Terrie and I looked forward to our trip to the Kentucky Lake cabins with Mom and Teddy. They'd let us drive the boat and go fishing. Terrie was eight years old and I was ten—so we were always ready for an adventure.

One time at the lake, Mom asked, "Do you girls want to go swimming?"

Even though we didn't know how to swim, we shouted, "Yeah!" thinking we were going to a swimming pool.

Little did we know, Mom and Teddy had other plans. They strapped us in life vests, tied ropes around our waists, and threw us overboard yelling, "Swim!"

I had a *fit* ... screaming, flailing my arms and legs, desperately trying not to touch anything in the lake waters below. I was terrified of snakes and all the other stuff that could be lurking. Even after eventually taking swimming lessons at the YMCA, I'm still scared of water to this day. But regardless, I loved Teddy. That didn't change.

\* \* \*

Teddy and Mom eventually broke up. My mother drank and was a drug addict so life was always changing. She verbally and physically abused us. My dad, also an alcoholic, owned his own bar. So, I pretty much grew up in bars one way or another. Not having Teddy to watch over us anymore, Mom would leave us with people we didn't know and be gone for days. We never knew where she went.

One night, Mom rushed out the door of Tammy's\* house for her night shift at Ireland's, a restaurant in Nashville, Tennessee. This time she left us with Rick\*, Tammy's boyfriend. Terrie and I lay down in the living room, eventually falling asleep to the hum of the TV. But my slumber didn't last long. I awoke during the night to Rick hovering over me.

"Shhhhhh," he whispered as he saw my eyes spread wide in fear.

He watched us from time to time, but had never molested me until then. The following day, after Momma left again for work, Rick grabbed my arm, pulling me to the side of the house.

"You'd better not tell nobody what we did. That's our secret," he said.

"I'm gonna tell my momma," I responded in defiance.

"If you tell your momma, I'm going to get your little sister like that," Rick said.

And that was that. It was forever locked within me.

\* \* \*

Things changed after that. When I was twelve, Mom would leave Terrie with a babysitter and take me to Ireland's with her and Aunt Pat. The staff would let me help roll the silverware. Then they would reward me with Ireland's famous steak and biscuits and a little chocolate pie.

At closing time, I'd drink a little with the waitresses and my aunt. Then one day they took me into the bathroom. I always assumed they were just smoking cigarettes back there, until a joint was put in my hand. I liked the way it made me feel. I didn't have to think. I could escape from anything and anybody.

## Getting the Best of Me

Around age fourteen my drug habit began. Momma was letting me drink with her at the beer joints. I didn't hang around many people, especially not guys. The only guy I ever really trusted was Teddy. I was always happy to see him. He was still a bouncer at one of the bars in the area, so he'd let me in to drink. He probably shouldn't have, but I thought he was just looking out for me, which was desperately needed.

Ireland's was the last job Mom had. She continued to go to bars, though I wasn't sure how she made her money. We moved to the projects and had to get on welfare. By this time, our family had grown to five girls and one boy. Being the oldest, I had more weight on my shoulders, trying to help Mom and my siblings whenever I could. You had to be rough and tough to survive where we lived. You had to fight. I let fear get the best of me at times. I made some bad decisions.

\* \* \*

I had my first son, Jason, at the age of sixteen. Jason's father, Mike, was twenty-eight years old at the time. My second and third sons, Joseph and Jonathon, were born several years later by another man, also named Mike. I lived in housing projects off of Shelby Avenue for a while, and then moved into a trailer next to my mom in Fairview. France, a power-solutions manufacturing company, hired me to work the night-shift, so I practically never saw my kids because of the odd hours.

My addictions picked up speed. What started as a pot habit led to using crack. I swallowed lots of pills, drank daily, and even as a teenager, shot up drugs. I knew I needed help, so I turned to the

Vanderbilt Institute for Treatment of Addiction (VITA) program. VITA's staff sent me to admit myself into the Gateway Recovery Center in Fort Smith, Arkansas. My kids were divided up to live with my mom and two sisters.

At the end of my ten-month stay, Mom came to pick me up. I eagerly swung open the car door, relieved to go home and finally see my kids again. But instead of jumping on the road, Momma pulled out a joint and eased into her seat. Her thumb swiped the lighter and within seconds, my temptation was stretched out in front of me.

"You want a hit?" she asked.

I resisted at first, but my will-power crumbled. All of that time spent in recovery for nothin'. I was back to square one.

I clearly needed to remove myself from my surroundings. So, I moved to South Carolina to work as a nanny. However, this didn't work out as well as planned. Drugs still had a part of my life, only their role had changed. This time, I sold drugs for my employer. Then my hole sunk deeper. The police lights flashed in my rear-view mirror.

"I'm going to need you to breathe into this," the officer stated.

I already knew where I was headed. A cold jail cell welcomed me after the sting of the DUI.

"You've got to go, Penny," my boss said, dropping bus money in my hand to get me back to Nashville. Apparently, leaving my home town wasn't going to solve my problems; they would follow me anywhere.

\* \* \*

I wasn't getting any better, so I turned to Choose You\*, a recovery facility specializing in mental illness, to try to get sober. I moved into one of their apartments while earning an income waiting tables at T.G.I. Fridays, as well as working part time as an event crowd-controller in downtown Nashville. However, Choose You didn't have many restrictions. We only had to sign papers agreeing not to do any illegal drugs. But alcohol was legal. I found the catch 22. I drank as much as I wanted, knowing they couldn't touch me.

I couldn't get it together. I still had great connections, knowing everybody who smoked or sold pills. One of my run-ins with the police was even taped and aired on an episode of *Cops*. However, Keri Seay, an employee at Choose You, shined like a light in the darkness. Keri always listened without judgment. But when the moment came to speak truth, she didn't sugar-coat anything. And then there was Donna Grayer, another employee I could confide in. I trusted her whole-heartedly.

"I'm not like these people here, Donna," I told her.

Everyone at Choose You was on different types of psychiatric medication for their mental illnesses. Some were abusing their medications. Some were over-medicated. But not me. The doctors diagnosed me as bi-polar/manic-depressant, telling me I needed medication, though I tried to convince them otherwise. I walked into my appointments, collected the meds, and took them straight home to toss in the garbage. I knew what my problem was, and it wasn't mental illness.

Stolen Moments

Mom was still struggling, receiving breathing treatments at her regular doctor's visits. She was diagnosed with lung cancer and told that she needed to quit smoking immediately. But of course, she didn't. The following week, she returned from her appointment with the news.

"The doctor gave me six months to live."

"Oh, yeah? You're stubborn. You'll live a whole lot longer than that!" I responded with a forced smile.

About two weeks later, I was working my T.G.I. Fridays shift when I got a call from my sister Tina.

"You need to get over here—get over here now!"

"What's going on?" I responded.

"We don't think she's going to make it the rest of the day, Penny."

"What do you *mean*? The doctors said she had six months and it hasn't even been two *weeks* yet!"

By the time I got to Momma's house, she was already gone. I

think she just gave up. She didn't believe she had any reason left to fight. There were things I said to her when times were tough. I had only wished for just a few moments with her before she passed. Now all I had was regret.

## Life under the Bridge

I looked around at my reality. I was homeless, living under a bridge in Nashville. The ground beneath me was littered with broken beer bottles. It reeked of pee and crap everywhere, also serving as a bathroom. Unless I passed out from using, there was no time for sleep—the scurrying rats and people with hidden motives kept me awake. I had to be on my toes. No one else would watch my back but me.

One of my dealers had a CB radio in his car. He used it to find his next client, either to sell dope or to prostitute his old lady. So I bought myself a CB radio, hopefully guaranteeing my own clients and ultimately, my next fix. Pretty soon I had the process down: "Hey trucker, my name is Candy. What's your twenty?" I prostituted myself to make money and use all over again. This brought me at least sixty percent of my clients.

The terrifying moments were endless. I tried to keep my eyes open and hang in a crowd, but that couldn't always save me. Even if I wasn't causing the trouble, sometimes I was just at the wrong place at the wrong time. I've been beaten so badly I ended up in the hospital. Among the beatings, I was robbed, raped twice, arrested four times, and got three DUIs. But regardless of the toll it took on me, I went back to the bridge. And I stayed there ... for approximately ten years.

> *"We either make ourselves miserable, or we make ourselves strong. The amount of work is the same."*
> ~Carlos Castaneda

*  *  *

I was ashamed of what I had become—of the place I called home. But despite that, when my son Joseph came to town for a visit, I brought him to the bridge. I told him things—things I'd rather not repeat. Things I desperately wish to forget. My words shredded him. Guilt and regret was instant.

"Wait. Joseph, I'm sorry! Come back over here. Talk to me!" I begged.

But he refused. The next morning I woke up knowing I had to get him out of there. We stayed at a motel for a few days, but the damage had already been done. Joseph returned to Florida to live with his dad, trying to leave behind everything I put him through. Though, I doubt that was possible.

*  *  *

I needed to escape from the bridge. I stayed at another treatment facility called The Elam Center for forty-five days. In daily support groups we were encouraged to share things about ourselves, although I didn't share everything. Then once a week I shoveled through my past with a counselor. I could tell her anything, things I would hold back in group meetings.

"I'm going to the Magdalene[7] program soon," I said to her. (Another woman at Elam had recently decided to go there.)

"Yeah, so many of them do. A lot don't make it because they promise this and that, but they never change," she said.

"What do you mean, 'they don't change'?" I asked.

"They tell me anything just to get where they want to go."

Of course—empty promises just to find the next fix.

With a confident smile I said, "Ooohhh, well … I'm gonna make a liar out of you."

I knew I'd make it someday. I had the drive in my heart to make it happen and was determined to prove her wrong.

---

[7] Magdalene: http://www.thistlefarms.org/index.php/about-magdalene

\* \* \*

There he was again, glaring at me from his elevated seat at the head of the Mental Health Court room. Judge Einstein knew me well, and not from shining moments. He was becoming fed up with me, trying time and time again to pull me from my messes. He took me to a homeless function, contacted my sister, and even called Joseph and my ex-old man, Mike, in Florida.

"We can't do nothing with her," Mike said.

None of them knew how to help me.

But Judge Einstein saw something within me that I didn't. He handed me the number for the Magdalene program treatment center that had been on my mind since Elam. Maybe this was it. Maybe this was the sign that I needed. I had the number in my hand. No excuse not to call.

"Well, I've done all I can, Penny. It's up to you now. I don't want to see you in my courtroom again, I'm sick of looking at 'cha," he said.

His hand stretched toward me, putting money in mine.

"*Promise* me you won't use this for your next fix—only food," he said.

Somehow I managed to buy both. But when I woke up the next morning, things were different for some reason. I didn't want to live like this anymore … and I meant it this time. For thirty years I had given in to my addiction—enough to last me a lifetime. Somehow, Judge Einstein lit a fire within me that had been out for as long as I can remember. I was done.

> **"Life doesn't give us what we deserve.**
> **Life gives us what we go claim."**
> ~Stephen Pierce

## Magdalene

By this time, I had been to so many treatment centers it wasn't even funny. But that didn't stop me from giving Magdalene a shot. I approached Donna Grayer. Donna had left Choose You and was now the Assistant Director of Magdalene.

"You have room for me, Donna?" I asked.

"Well, okay ... let's see," she responded. Magdalene almost always had a waiting list, so finding a spot this easily would be a miracle. "I have one spot open," she concluded. Pulling me aside, her eyebrows and forehead squished into one as she continued, "But Penny, we go way back. You know I love you, but there's no drinking in this house."

Donna wasn't about to let it happen a second time, as it had at Choose You.

"No drinking, Penny. I mean it. Don't let me catch you 'cause you'll be out."

I stared directly into her concrete eyes and said, "Donna, I'm done. I promise you."

Those may have been empty words to some people, but Donna was different. She gave me another chance. But more importantly, *I* needed to be different. I was determined, but lacked hope. I was going to relapse in my first year, I just *knew* it. But I soon found out this was unlike any other program.

> **"Strength doesn't come from what you can do. It comes from overcoming the things you once thought you couldn't."**
> *~Rikki Rogers*

## Told You So

Magdalene is a two-year program with four different phases. For the first six months I was an "Initiate." A team member did my initial assessment, documenting what I wanted to accomplish. Next, I was sent to an Intensive Out-Patient (IOP) facility for counseling and drug testing. Every type of doctor visit had to be done, including a visit to the Mental Health Co-op for a standard consultation. I sat in the freezing exam room, waiting for my evaluation results.

"I don't think you need medication, Penny," the doctor said.

"I don't think I need 'em either," I replied.

"You don't have issues in any of the areas I tested you for. You sound like you know what you want. So, I'm not going to prescribe you anything today."

"Can I get a second opinion to make sure?" I asked, still wanting to prove Choose You one-hundred-percent wrong.

"Absolutely," she said.

She sent me to another doctor who confirmed the exact same thing. I marched out the door with one destination in mind. My feet couldn't get me back to Magdalene fast enough. I needed to tell Donna!

"See, I told you I was different," I said with a grin.

\* \* \*

Those first few months, I didn't want to be there. I thought I knew everything. The staff was always telling me no. The rules were somewhat ridiculous. You couldn't have a job, cell phone, visitors other than family, or go anywhere by yourself. Some of the other women were hard-headed like me; advice or direction went in one ear and out the other. We all had different struggles. However, we were more alike than we could admit. I got along with my roommates, but that didn't mean it wasn't tough sharing space with so many others. I planned to stay in my shared bedroom as much as possible. That would save me.

But I couldn't hide in my room forever—Magdalene kept us busy. Not only did this keep us out of trouble, but also forced us to focus on recovery. During the weekdays, classes were given at the main house: Anger Management Class, Spirituality Class, Parenting Class, etc. I started to let myself *really* listen. One class here. One class there. Life slowly began to turn—to look different.

Then I walked into the Prostitution class. That was one of the *last* things I wanted to talk about. When living on the streets, the only way to make money was to prostitute. It brought so much shame. So much guilt. To forget that pain, I'd get high again. I never had goals. My only vision was getting another beer or taking a hit with the people under the bridge. Then, I'd have to sell my body again to make more money. An endless circle of bad choices. But now I was learning the truth. Prostituting was only a symptom of my addiction. I was making the choice. The circle needed to end.

\* \* \*

The second and third steps in the program are the "Postulant" and "Novitiate" phases. After completing a computer class at the Opportunities Industrialization Center (OIC), I started working at Thistle Farms[8] (Magdalene's social enterprise, specializing in making bath and body products) and saving money. I was so excited to see Keri Seay doing my check-in; she had left Choose You to work for Magdalene as Donna had.

"I'm here to help you set some goals, Penny. Do you want to go back to school? Do you want to save enough money to buy your own place someday? Do you want to get your GED?" she asked.

Whatever I decided, Keri and Donna found the support I needed. "You are all *smart* women," we were reminded.

My eyes shot up from their anchored spot on the floor. Smart? *Really?* I'd never been told that before.

By this time I could leave the property as long as I checked in with the staff, always making sure to return on time for curfew. The most important thing was to tell the truth. If we lied, the consequences would be waiting. Being honest about where I was going and what I was doing would get me further than any lie ever would.

Meanwhile, the women were always bickering, jumping into each other's faces. My "street senses" were still a big part of me. I meant what I said. If I said I'd lay my hands on someone, it wasn't a threat. I'd do it. There was no telling what might happen. I needed to avoid the chaos. So I stayed to myself, casually saying "hi" and "bye."

Ultimately, I told myself that if I stuck to the program and gave it a chance, life would get better. Time would tell.

---

[8] Thistle Farms: http://www.thistlefarms.org/

## Angel in Plain Clothes

I had to pinch myself. Two long years passed and I was finally hearing those words.

"Congratulations, Penny. You've reached the Candidate phase!"

I was an applicant to graduate! *I did it!* I was *free* ... from so many things. But it was more than just the structure of the program that made this work. Becca Stevens[9], founder of the Magdalene program and Thistle Farms, gave us the courage to believe. Many of the women had been sexually abused, so her story of being molested as a child connected with us. She trusted us when no one else would, not only to accomplish our goals, but to work at Thistle Farms, a company she built to support us.

Becca had a vision, not only for the program, but for the world— to *love without judgment*. But the women in Magdalene came from a completely different world. No one wanted to mess with people like us. We were far from perfect. Our guards were up and love didn't exist. But Becca made it her life mission to love us regardless of our pasts. At first it was hard to believe she was real. *Could this person—this place—really love me for me? And wait ... this is love?* Before then, love was a lie.

"Love Heals." That was Becca's motto. We learned what love is—to take it in and let it bloom. To not only let that love, hope, and trust reach us, but also change us. It was our job to live the example she provided. We couldn't just accept these gifts; giving them away was just as important. This would change us from the people we were, to the people we wanted to be.

> **"Wisdom is oftentimes nearer when we stoop than when we soar."**
> ~William Wordsworth

\* \* \*

For a very long time, I didn't believe in God. If there really was

---

[9] Becca Stevens: http://www.beccastevens.org/about-becca/

a God up there, why was He putting me through this? But Becca had a clear vision for the women of Magdalene in God's world. She connected stories from the Bible to what we had lived through. She explained to us how we currently viewed things, how to view them differently, and the possibilities that came with that. We were empowered. And slowly, my perspective changed.

I started to believe. I've realized there *is* a God. He's my God, and His name is Jesus. I'm letting Him into my life again, giving my worries over to Him. I had to surrender every day to take my desires away, asking God for the strength and guidance that I needed to stay clean. I surrendered to change, which I never knew was necessary. I changed my ideas about myself and my life, realizing that I *was* worth it. I can resist picking up drugs with God on my side. He gives me strength to see the other side. You have to get through the storm to see the sunshine.

\* \* \*

The Magdalene program is a gift. It's changing things, giving people like us a chance. Sometimes that's what we need to keep up the fight—someone to hold your hand, still caring about you no matter what you've done. To my surprise, I did not relapse that year or any other year. Life had shown up in the midst of my misery.

I have no idea how Becca does what she does, but that's what makes her so special. She gets her strength from God to pass on to us. She's a blessing. My angel in plain clothes.

## A True Escape ... to the Other Side

We drove down Gallatin Road Main Street. I used to hang out there a lot, walking the streets and making connections. My Home Group supported me as we stopped at a store where a lot of my old friends used.

"Hi Penny. You look so good!" I heard.

It's extremely tough to think about how I left them behind. Now, I often wonder what they're doing. Are they in jail, passed away, or God help them if they've been killed?

* * *

My body shot straight up from my bed as my lungs gasped for air. Sweat mixed with my tears as they dropped to my chest. *It wasn't real! It's okay,* I told myself. *I'm okay.*

This still happens, my past creeping into my dreams. Sometimes I wonder how it would be if I used again. *Could I handle it? Could I just do it and quit?* But I don't want to go back to that world. God pulls me from my nightmare. He gets me out of bed. I thank Him every day for that, starting the day with a prayer asking Him to take away my desires. I make the daily choice to surrender, knowing that I'm powerless over people, places, and circumstances, accepting things for what they are.

> **"No time is so well spent in every day as that which we spend upon our knees."**
> *~J.C. Ryle*

Others will bring you down if you let them. Today I can choose the company I keep to prevent myself from being miserable, and I choose Thistle Farms. People count on me. I have a key to the front door and am trusted to handle large amounts of money. Nobody is looking over my shoulder. I can't tell you how good that feels! But even with all of my work responsibilities, I can't forget about the responsibilities I have to myself and my family, just to continue breathing and living, knowing every choice I made before finding Magdalene had pushed me toward death.

It took a lot of hard work and a lot of loving hearts, but I made it. Using again is not an option. If I do it once, it will happen again. I'm not willing to take that chance. People look up to me now and I won't let them down. So today, at this very minute, I'm going to continue fighting. Life is a lot easier on this side of the street.

## The Breath of Freedom

I completed the Magdalene program on December 5, 2010, and have been sober since October 22, 2008. I have learned everything I could from the program and now I have to continue to live it each and every day. I've worked at Thistle Farms since May 25, 2009. I'm now the manager of the paper facility and the supervisor of the packing facility. I have such relief that I have a job that I love and a safe place to live. I've accomplished so many of my goals: I've saved money and paid off my fines; I've made amends with my kids; I'm currently working on getting my GED and won't let anything stop me from making that happen.

My choices have affected my children and their lives, but I know that I can now love them the way that I should have. Despite any pain that I have caused those I love, each and every day they inspire me to keep trying, keep fighting, and keep loving—if not for me, for them. I'm making a difference in my family by breaking the cycle. Now it's time to enter the next phase of my life. I have a new vision, and trust me, it's a bright one.

\* \* \*

It's hard to offer advice to others. We're all different ages, with different experiences and struggles. It's common to become hard-headed, believing that you know what's best for yourself. However, if I were to give advice to an addict who is willing to take it, I would tell her/him:

*~Continue your meetings.*

*~Remember, there will be good days and bad days. But no matter what those days look like, you don't have to use drugs or alcohol.*

*~If you need to talk to someone in the middle of the night—call.*

*~Live day by day, praying for guidance and strength. Let God be in control instead of you; He already has it planned out for us anyway.*

*~Love yourself always.*

*~Be true to yourself and God; feel the surrender of all your burdens being lifted away by Him. Never pick them back up.*

*~Even when no one is looking, do what is right.*

*~Believe in yourself at all times; never give up.*

Life is what you make of it. If you're negative all the time, your life will be negative. If you work hard, things do get better. If it takes two years or four years—it doesn't matter. When a day doesn't go as planned, restart and keep moving. Do your best to work through the problems that arrive instead of running from them. No matter what, you don't have to use. God is faithful and if you have the will, anything is possible. Freedom lives, users don't.

> **"Let us hold fast the confession of our hope without wavering, for He who promised is faithful;"**
> Hebrews 10:23
> (NASB)

As the saying goes, "Don't give up five minutes before the miracle happens." We are blessed with miracles every day that we take for granted. It is a miracle to wake up in the morning. It's a miracle to breathe. I have my license, a car to drive, and my own house to live in. Those are the blessings from a miracle. It's a true miracle that I'm standing here today, telling my story. So, after everything I've lived through, still coming out on the other side with miracles in hand, how could I *not* believe in hope?

> **"We must accept finite disappointment,**
> **but we must never lose infinite hope."**
> ~*Martin Luther King, Jr.*

## Despite Thorns

The Thistle is a tough weed covered by thorns, needing very little water to survive. Often you'll see one growing through the cracks in hard concrete, in fields, or by railroad tracks. One seed can produce a million thistles. We start out in the Magdalene program just like that thistle. We come from the street, tough as nails. We think we know it all, now needing to adapt to our surroundings. We believe no one has the right to tell us anything, and that we are the only ones with our best interests in mind. Our thorns keep everyone at a distance. However, the thistle, like us, eventually begins to bloom despite its thorns, producing a soft, bright purple flower. Just because you come from thorns doesn't mean you can't produce something soft and beautiful.

> **"Love yourself—accept yourself—forgive yourself—and**
> **be good to yourself, because without you the rest of us**
> **are without a source of many wonderful things."**
> ~*Leo F. Buscaglia*

*Margaret Ann "Penny" Hall passed away on June 2, 2015,*
*breaking the hearts of many; however, not before teaching*
*all of us what it means to truly wear the face of hope.*

*Names or locations have been changed to protect those involved.

## Reflection Questions

1.  In an interview with NPR, Becca Stevens states, "No one went to the streets by themselves. It took a lot of failed systems and a lot of brokenness to get them out there." What played a role in leading Penny to live on the streets as an addict?

2.  In order to overcome her many fears, Penny needed to confront them. What are you afraid of today that could be confronted? Ask yourself, what are the *symptoms* of your fear, as opposed to the *fear itself*?

3.  Sometimes we tend to allow certain habits or people in our lives to become crutches, or even addictions. Are you relying on something or someone in your life more than necessary?

# Producing Something Beautiful: Seeds of Growth

Think of someone in need and reach out.

Judge Einstein, Becca Stevens, and countless others were instrumental in supporting Penny's road to stability and healing. In our own environments, we have opportunities to provide a helping hand, a source of light—not only to our friends and family, but anyone we pass on the street or meet in a chat room. Helping others doesn't have to be accomplished by way of substantial donation. While donating materials, food, or money is helpful, reaching out to another can be equally impactful through small measures:

*~donating our time*
*~helping a neighbor*
*~sending a thoughtful card*
*~sharing our stories—providing guidance and encouragement*
*~holding a door open for another to walk through*
*~lending an ear to someone who just needs to be heard*
*~thanking a soldier for selflessly risking his/her life for our country*
*~offering an unexpected compliment*
*~sending up a prayer in the quiet of the day*
*~just offering a smile*

> **"When God's people are in need, be ready to help them.**
> **Always be eager to practice hospitality."**
> Romans 12:13
> (NLT)

Can you imagine the change that would occur in others and us if everyone took a moment to do at least one thoughtful action every day? Our world would be a very different place. Leave your legacy—not in possessions or accolades—but in moments. Moments that matter.

> **"The greatest use of life is to spend it for something that will outlast it."**
> ~William James

\* \* \*

**"Very truly I tell you, whoever believes in me will do the works I have been doing, and they will do even greater things than these, because I am going to the father. And I will do whatever you ask in my name, so that the Father may be glorified in the Son."**
*John 14:12-13*
*(NIV)*

In the verse above, Jesus declares the forecast for those that follow him: We shall "do even greater things than these." To clarify, these aren't "things" for selfish and fruitless earthly benefits, but are actions mirroring those of Jesus. Actions that glorify our Father and radiate His love. Actions that involve sacrifice, exuding a gracious and joyful spirit. I can't even fathom doing greater things than Jesus Himself. However, we are designed with the power to do so. We just need to take that first step. And if we allow Him, He will lead us.

# CHAPTER 5
## Chappy's Story ~ The Perpetual Spark

*"He must trust, and he must have faith. And so he builds, because what is building, and rebuilding and rebuilding again, but an act of faith?"*
~Dave Eggers

After a long work week, Friday came to a close as I made my usual stop at Parker's in New Orleans, a high-class bar where businessmen congregated. As I entered, I immediately noticed a new girl behind the bar.

"We've got a new bartender today!" I said.

"Oh yeah, her name is Starr," the owner replied.

"Hey Starr, honey, how about a Jack on the rocks?" I asked with a smile.

"In a minute, I'm *busy*," she replied, packed with annoyance.

Finally, Starr reached out and shot a glass of Jack straight down the bar, landing smack-dab in front of me. "How's that for your *black jack*?" she said.

"That's fine, darlin', thank you!" And that's how I met my beautiful wife.

Of course, it took some sweet-talking on my part. Though I was just having fun that day, not meaning any harm, I may not have made the best first impression. A dozen roses to express my apologies, several trips back to Parker's to get acquainted, two "dates" where I had the pleasure of taking out Starr and her girlfriend for a night on the town, and many laughs later, I finally convinced Starr to let me take her on a date alone. We hit it off big time and the rest is history.

I was twenty-nine years old when we married in 1983. On our honeymoon, we spent a week in London, followed by a week in Paris. I'd never been to Europe before, so we were really excited. We wanted to see everything. In London, we ran around, partying until we couldn't go anymore, eventually dropping from exhaustion. We then took off for our week in France with plans to do the exact same thing; although, I had a specific location in mind.

Mumm's Cordon Rouge champagne, made in Reims, France, had been "our champagne" since our very first date.

"We've got to go there!" I exclaimed.

So of course, Starr and I boarded the train in Paris, fully ready for our next destination: The House of G.H.Mumm's.

Reims is a charming small town with little shops and cafés decorating the streets.

As we settled in at our table for lunch, I knew our first order would be a no-brainer: "Let's have two glasses of Mumm's Cordon Rouge!"

Unfortunately, the food menu was a bit harder to decipher, scribbled on a chalkboard entirely in French. Starr and I had no idea what was being offered. So we did the only thing we could do: Starr said, "I'll have number *un* (one), *s'il vous plait*," and I followed with, "I'll have a number *deux* (two), *s'il vous plait*." Simple enough.

To our delight, our mystery lunch was amazing! Overflowing with flavor and cooked to perfection. After the waiter warmed up to us, he slowly revealed that he spoke a little English.

"What exactly *is* this?" I asked.

"Your wife, she has ze veal. Ze veal."

"Oh! That was delightful!" Starr said.

"And what did I have?" I asked.

"Oh, you have ze lamb's testicles."

I let out a loud, barrel of laughter. "You are kidding me! Well ... they were delicious!" I learned my lesson from that point on, opening my mind further to the art of cuisine.

I fell in love with the culture in Europe. Food is culture and culture is food. I was completely absorbed in it. Every meal was an event. After those two weeks, my heart changed. Cooking hadn't necessarily become a *new* love, but it was definitely developing from a spark of passion into a blazing flame.

> *"It is possible at any age to discover a lifelong desire you never knew you had."*
> ~Robert Brault

## Igniting a Flame

Until I was about eight years old, we had a summer house on the bay in Fairhope Point Clear, Alabama. I couldn't wait to get there each year! We practically lived on the beach—fishing, crabbing, hunting, and swimming. In the middle of a hot, cloud-free day, my brother and I were in our typical location, playing on the beach of Mobile Bay.

"Don't move!" my brother said.

Goosebumps covered me as a subtle, yet determined cluster of legs inched up my back. I turned toward the water just in time to see millions of crabs making their way up the beach.

"IT'S JUBILEEEEEEEEE!" we roared.

A jubilee is when the sea and fresh water are positioned just right, forcing sea life to emerge onto the beach with the tide, seeking an increase in oxygen[10]. More often than not, it would take place in the middle of the night when the tides would change. Fish, crab, shrimp—everything seized the sand. At Battle's Wharf, a giant bell would ring as someone shouted, "Jubilee!"

Everyone dashed up and down the beach with gas lanterns. They'd toss the fish into a basket, scoop up the crabs with tongs or gig flounder. It only lasted about an hour, so we had to move

---

[10] May, Edwin B. "Extensive Oxygen Depletion in Mobile Bay, Alabama." Limnology and Oceanography XVIII (1973): 365. Print.

quickly. Because I was so young, Mom didn't want me out at 3:00 a.m. running up and down the beach after sea creatures. So instead I would be in the kitchen with her, cleaning the fish, boiling crabs, and peeling shrimp. If we caught it, we had to eat it. That was the rule.

## Fresh–There Was No Other Way

I was a guided child, being the youngest of five kids. Mom, from Jamaica, New York, was a very good cook. My parents met and resided for some time in the West Indies in the Caribbean. Sadly, my father, a British Consul in Mobile, Alabama, died when I was three years old from prostate cancer. I never really got to know him. My mother, a school teacher, died at the age of eighty-two from kidney failure, but not before she had a chance to instill many great lessons and values.

Living in such diverse locations allowed my mother to have a lot of different influences in her cooking. She cooked a complete breakfast every single day before school. Scrambled eggs, grits, toast—the works. My lunch at school could be a roasted lamb sandwich with mint jelly, fruit, and homemade dessert. What was cereal or fried bologna? We honestly never had it. Nothing fried. She didn't believe in foods like these. We always had traditional, wholesome ingredients with lots of vegetables. Real food made with love.

My mother got a job teaching at St. Lawrence the Martyr, so we moved to New Orleans from Mobile at the end of my fourth-grade year. The New Orleans culture had a completely new influence on me. I began my fifth-grade year with many surprises in store. My old school didn't even have a cafeteria. Much to my surprise, not only did St. Lawrence have one, but every day the ladies made breakfast *and* lunch, entirely from scratch. In the morning the kids would eat homemade cinnamon rolls and fresh fruit. And the coffee! This was my first experience with coffee, specifically Café Du Monde, coffee with chicory, served with half milk, half coffee. I'd dunk my cinnamon roll and savor the deliciousness.

We would arrive at school around 7:00 a.m.—not an ounce of life in the classrooms. I had absolutely nothing to do, so I began helping the ladies prepare breakfast.

"Morning, John! You ready to help? How about you grab the eggs for us?"

They took me under their wing, allowing me to assist in any way I could. While my mother finished her work at the end of the day, I'd help prepare for the next day's lunch as well. This was my first experience cooking for mass amounts of people. I absolutely loved it.

## Tug-of-War

In high school, I continued to be enamored with food, experimenting with anything I could to make a dish fantastic. Cooking, however, was only one of my passions. I was also a big music fan, becoming captain of the band all four years. On top of that, I joined the school paper, as well as the Business Department. Despite my many interests, business emerged as a large focal point.

I worked six days a week at the Exxon gas station starting when I was fifteen years old. After school, I'd arrive at work at 4:00 in the afternoon, working until 11:00 that night. On the fourth day, they made me shift manager, supervising guys who were fifty or sixty years old. I appreciated the guys working for me, often hosting card games in the back-bay after hours.

By eighteen, I was working on all kinds of different ventures, getting a head start on my future in the business world. I'd buy a house, renovate it, and resell it successfully. I also tarped trucks for The Gypsum Association. For ten dollars, I would have the truck loaded with Gypsum products, tarped, in position, and ready to go. I was working extremely hard, completing sixty to seventy trucks a day.

I staggered through the door after a long, rigorous work-day and was greeted by my mother placing an envelope in my hand. Loyola University, New Orleans. I sliced through the crisp white seal and yanked out its contents. A full scholarship for music. In high school, music was such a big part of me. But when it came down to music as a profession, I just couldn't see it. So, much to everyone's surprise, including mine, I turned it down. Business school at Loyola was my path.

\* \* \*

While attending college, I worked for Delta Steamship Lines. The whole process of international shipping fascinated me. So I began my pursuit! At the age of twenty-one, I graduated with a Bachelor of Arts degree in International Commerce, and two Certificates of Completion for International Traffic & Transportation Management, and Advanced Traffic. By the age of twenty-seven, I became the General Manager of T.R. Spedden, Inc., Shipping Agents with a Federal Maritime Commission License, having offices in New Orleans and Houston. Mr. T.R. Spedden (fondly referred to as Mr. Speedy) sold the company to me for only 1,000 dollars—a check which for some reason he never cashed.

I attended amazing parties on board ships from all over the world. Realizing I could combine two of my passions, business and entertainment, I didn't waste any time becoming a shipping agent so I could throw my own parties. We'd invite those who had cargo onboard and I'd work with the chef to plan the perfect menu. However, one party aboard an Argentinean freighter stood out above the rest. Having formerly existed as a passenger ship, its caramel-colored teak and pool on the main deck were striking. A live band played as everyone feasted. Instead of typical finger sandwiches, the crew cooked beef on racks Argentinean style, right on top of the hatch covers (openings on the deck of the ship). Such a simple, yet killer event! I walked away that evening seeing things from a different angle—a "new" and unique way of entertaining.

**"Simplicity is the ultimate sophistication."**
~Leonardo Da Vinci

## A Change of Heart

After our honeymoon, Starr and I began building our life together in New Orleans. The majority of the time we lived in a house on City Park Avenue. Loving to throw dinner parties, we converted the front porch into a dining room overlooking City Park's dueling oaks. Eventually we also bought a house on the beach in Waveland, Mississippi, which we adored. It was an eight-sided house constructed from grain-stroked pine and cedar wood. Thankfully, I was able to negotiate a deal, permitting us to keep that house as a getaway on the weekends.

But in 1983, exports almost dropped. We were going through a huge recession, becoming almost completely an import economy. My business just about died, after it had been doing extremely well. I was crushed. However, Europe's imprint remained on my heart. Food had taken on a whole other dimension, opening my mind to larger horizons. I always enjoyed cooking, but never thought of actually getting into it from a business perspective ... until now.

I said to Starr, "You know, I've been thinking more and more about going into the restaurant business. I think I'd like to give it a shot here on the coast. Since we have the house in Waveland that we love so much, let's just move there full time and open a restaurant. Maybe we can get this to work!"

> *"You miss one hundred percent of the shots you don't take."*
> ~Wayne Gretzky

I had some money saved, so if this didn't succeed we would still have something to fall back on. It was a risk, but I was willing to take it. So, in 1984 I rented a 7-Eleven store-front that was a restaurant/bar conversion. The property was right on the gulf, overlooking Long Beach Harbor. Starr and I fixed it up, giving it a European feel. We tore down walls, painted, and added ceiling fans. Seating ninety people, the restaurant provided ample space. Among the seating options was a gorgeous wooden bar, extending the length of the whole restaurant.

On our opening day at Chappy's, I made sure to make a large pot of gumbo. To my horror, it ended up being the worst batch I had ever made in my *life*. I couldn't believe it! No time to throw it out and start again. We were scheduled to open at eleven o'clock and people were already lined up outside the door ready to pile in.

"I guess I'll just have to doctor it up with lots of seafood, a little extra hot sauce .... Maybe they'll like it!" I said. Fingers crossed.

Chappy's was absolutely packed. A standing-room-only opening! People waited to get in for lunch until two o'clock. Gumbo was selling like crazy! I'd been getting notes from the customers that read: *Best gumbo I've ever had in my life! Keep up the good work!* or *Can't wait to come back!* Absolutely stunned, I grabbed Starr at the end of lunch and shouted, "I love this dang business, even my screw-ups are great!"

Come dinner that night, I had made a new batch of gumbo, the dining room was perfectly set, and everything was raring to go. Once again, a line of people waited for a table until ten o'clock! I prepared fish, seasoned entrees, dressed plates, and dropped by my customer's tables at every "free" moment. I had sold out of everything in one day—trout, soft shells, frogs legs, you name it! But there wasn't a lot of time to celebrate. My trusty seafood suppliers, Debbie and Frank McNeil of Waveland Seafood Market, woke up at five o'clock the next morning to begin filleting fish. By the end of the second day we were completely sold out yet again!

> **"Light yourself on fire with passion and people will come from miles to watch you burn."**
> ~John Wesley

Three years after opening, Starr and I retired the original Chappy's and purchased an existing restaurant two blocks east on Highway 90. The restaurant seated 200 guests. It was made entirely from cypress with an expansive deck out front overlooking the beach. Oak tree limbs hung over the drive as cars approached the building, begging the kids to run back and climb its trunk while parents took pictures. White tablecloths, brass chandeliers, and a grand fireplace at each end of the dining room created the perfect ambiance.

Though I was never a trained chef, life's experiences taught me how to cook, developing recipes that no one else had. I loved having fun with people, letting them experience different creations. It was music to my ears when I'd hear, "Ooooh! That's the best thing I've ever had!" I honed my skills at every opportunity, studying with Julia Child in Venice and at the Ritz Escoffier in Paris. My passion continued to burn, never ceasing in its adventure.

My son, John, and daughter, Laura, were born and raised into this lifestyle. They grew up working in the restaurant, experiencing the business firsthand. Starr and I added on to our beautiful home. We added a pool, built a pier out front, and by the time we were done, we had four expansive acres right there on the beach. We made so many spectacular memories there with our family and friends, of course enduring what seemed like endless hurricanes along the way.

And then came Katrina.

Katrina, Not Your Average Hurricane

By the time 2005 came around, I had experienced at least fifty hurricanes. Hurricane Elena took everything inside the restaurant. I arrived after the storm to find all the glass completely blown out and the National Guard standing behind the bar eating my fresh oranges. The traffic light from the corner sat right on our dining room floor! But thankfully, our structure had never been destroyed. The damage was always repairable.

The Friday night before Katrina, I hosted a grand gourmet dinner. At *Moonlight on the Bay*, a fundraiser for Hancock Medical Center, Dr. Robert Gagne's auction bid won a dinner for eight in our home. I couldn't have been more excited! During dinner, one of the attendees received frequent updates on Katrina, due to his relatively high position within the Mississippi Power Company. But the message from his last call was a bit of a surprise. "Jim Cantore is covering the story in Biloxi. The hurricane's taking a turn. It looks like it's coming into the gulf-coast area," he said.

Everyone knew that when Jim Cantore from *The Weather Channel* showed up, you were in big trouble. Yet, this news didn't even faze me. It had to be a mistake. We'd seen the weather report earlier—the storm was scheduled to move west. So behaving normally, I moved forward planning for Saturday's business.

Around ten o'clock on Saturday night, I got a call from my friend Charles. "The water's rising, Chappy. This hurricane's going to hit us. I *know* it."

This was before the weathermen had predicted it themselves. Trusting my friend's intuition, we started securing the restaurant and our home that very night. I decided we wouldn't open for brunch on Sunday, we would just wait it out. But that wasn't going to stop us from attending mass.

St. Clare Church began at 11:00 a.m., right on schedule. Both of my children attended St. Clare School and Laura had also been baptized within the church, so I loved getting involved. I showed up ready to play guitar and lead the children's choir as I did every week. I looked forward to these moments and wasn't about to let a storm stop me.

That morning, the weatherman made their announcement: "It looks like the hurricane is going to come close to the gulf coast, at the very least."

Nothing was certain though, so everybody was pretty freaked out. The moment the service ended, the entire congregation instantly scattered to prepare. That day was my last at St. Clare's.

\* \* \*

Charles and his brother-in-law, Carl, arrived at our house ready for action. "We're ready to put the plywood on! They're showing a direct hit. It's supposed to double-back and cut right in, landing on our doorstep," Charles declared.

But that only gave us twenty-four hours. No time to waste. We spent the entire day securing everything as if it were a regular hurricane. We boarded the house with complete sheets of plywood surrounding the entire structure, then returning to the restaurant to add a few finishing touches. Our boat was next on the list, transporting the forty-three foot cypress trawler to a friend's pier on the Jordan River, as it had been many hurricanes before.

Ron called from Nashville to check in on us. He and his wife Louise were very close friends with our family, even having their own bedroom in our home during visits.

"Why don't y'all just come and stay up here? You can wait out the storm in Nashville and when the coast is clear y'all can just go back down." Louise would be out of town playing bridge with some friends for the whole week so Ron was excited about having the company. "We'll have a Labor Day party. It'll be great!" he said.

"That does sound great, Ron, but I think we may need to stay a bit closer to home in order to clean up our property when the storm ends. We appreciate the offer, though," I replied.

That night, we made sure the convertible Corvette, convertible Mustang, and Harley were all protected in the garage. We then packed up our remaining two cars with necessities required to ride out the storm. There was never a need to take a lot with us—some clothes and maybe a few bottles of really special, expensive wine. We had collected many precious items from all around the world: original Alice Mosley's, crystals, Faberge eggs, chandeliers, and endless antiques. We left it all in place, thinking we'd be back as usual, picking up where life had left off.

The aftermath of a typical hurricane usually isn't too bad. You come home, clean up, and replace a few shingles. Once your power comes back on, everything's back to normal. We really had *no idea* what we were in for.

## Vacancy in Hattiesburg

Hotel vacancies didn't exist, all the way to Wisconsin. Everything was closed. So Sunday night, we took off toward a friend's house in Hattiesburg. Scared to death of the storm, he was fleeing to stay with friends farther north, wanting us to babysit his property during the hurricane. Hattiesburg was approximately eighty miles inland—about a ninety-minute drive. So Starr, John, Laura, John's friend Chester (whose mother worked for the power company, busy on storm duty), our two dogs, and I jumped on the road to safety.

Exhausted from storm preparation, we crashed into a deep sleep upon making it to the house, only to awake bright and early Monday morning for a storm-status update. Our focus fixed on the television. We spotted the eye of the hurricane. It was positioned *directly* on top of our house in Waveland. Reported wind speed was 240 miles an hour with the water level already reaching approximately fifty-five feet. Being an hour inland, it took a little longer for the storm to find us. Yet we weren't excluded. Darkness hit. Power was lost. We were done—cut off from any details or communication with civilization. Katrina had moved over us.

* * *

A hurricane is its own beast of a storm. There are hours of prolonged destruction. At first, presenting itself as only a bad thunderstorm, then escalating in severity, appearing to never cease until the eye makes its way over you. The atmosphere becomes very quiet. Very still. Absolutely eerie. Approximately ten minutes of calm passes until the turmoil hits you from the opposite direction just as bad as it had before the eye approached (due to the counter-clockwise wind).

The eye of the storm hovered over us. Unnatural serenity covered Hattiesburg. We held our breath, knowing this peaceful camouflage would soon end. Sure enough, the storm thrust itself back toward the house, popping trees as if they had no business standing in the first place.

"Oh man, this is a *storm*," I declared as I stared out the window in shock.

Katrina finally passed, leaving us to survey our surroundings. With the electricity still out and sundown approaching, we only had about two hours of sunlight before inevitable darkness. Trees had fallen everywhere, on top of everything. But miraculously, everything looked okay! John and I borrowed a neighbor's chainsaw to cut down the trees that had crashed onto the house. Evidently, without their support, the roof would have shifted due to the low pressure and eventually torn off completely.

We were unable to receive updates on the storm. No power. No TV. No radio. No broadcasting whatsoever. Alabama, Mississippi, and Louisiana were all black. Three solid states … out. Learning from experience, the last thing John and I had done before we left for Hattiesburg was fill up our gas tanks. Having plenty of fuel for the cars, John, Chester, and I awoke at sunrise and took off. It was time to check out the aftermath.

## With Our Own Eyes

My sturdy Expedition was elevated pretty high off the ground, so we'd be okay on most of the rough roads in our future. I spun through the radio stations as we drove, hoping to hear a voice—any voice that could connect us to home. The civil defense radio coming out of Jackson, Mississippi was all I could find: "The power is currently out across the whole state of Mississippi. It looks like it's a catastrophic…."

Nothing we didn't already know. Clearly, we were officially on our own.

During the second half of the storm, the wind had shifted directions, fiercely blowing east, causing the trees along the interstate to collapse directly on top of the southbound lanes. The trees on the opposite side followed the same course, falling away from the northbound lanes. This left me with only one option—maneuvering down the opposite side of the typical interstate route. Evidently I wasn't alone. A state trooper followed me, as well as a little Nissan truck sticking close behind the trooper. My Expedition's path was the gateway to the road that lay ahead. But sadly, we were the only ones. Other than the state trooper following us, there were no state police anywhere, no civil defense ... nothing. Everybody was in really bad trouble.

While navigating through a few shortcuts, we cleared trees obstructing our path and eventually made it to Kiln, Mississippi, about ten to fifteen miles from the coast. Kiln is near the high end of where the bay starts, getting up into the countryside. It hadn't seen as much water, but that didn't mean they didn't have destruction. A massive blanket of trees covered the ground. Occasionally people stood aimlessly on the side of the road, mouths gaping as their gazes shuffled across the horizon, no doubt trying to swallow the nightmare before them.

The farther we traveled the harder it became. Water now covered the interstate, though slowly receding.

"I'm goin'! We've got to see what's going on," I said as I accelerated ahead.

I took my time, knowing that being too hasty could get me into trouble. We didn't know how bad our surroundings would continue to get, but slowly, reality swept upon us. Dead cows. Boats lay upended across and alongside the road. Debris as far as the eye could see. As I drove underneath the overpass of Interstate 10, something caught my eye. The water line, still visible on its cement supports, indicated a depth of approximately forty-five feet, nearly covering the overpass entirely. Yet shockingly, we were still about three miles inland. I knew in that moment ... everything was gone.

## Catching Our Breath

We continued down Highway 603. Not a soul in sight until we came to our little town of Waveland. On our right, the dilapidated Holiday Inn remained, providing safety from the high waters to those decorating its roof. However, the view to the left sledgehammered our hope. I blinked several times, hoping my eyes were deceiving me. A dead body appeared to be floating in the empty K-Mart parking lot. My heartbeat pounded through every limb. *Dear God, no.*

\* \* \*

Our first stop was Chester's house—flooded but still intact. Hoping to retrieve a pair of boots or clothing, we forced our legs through the water. It just wasn't going to happen. Katrina owned our possessions now. As we climbed in the SUV to head to our next destination, Chester's eyes narrowed, mirroring the road ahead. Their focus clearly wasn't on the four walls we were leaving behind; his concern and heart remained with his mom, still serving on emergency storm duty. We could only hope she was safe.

By the time we arrived at our street, Waveland Avenue, off of Interstate 90, the water had receded, allowing us to fully observe the destruction. Tree trunks and limbs lay everywhere. Houses lay in the middle of the road. Shards of glass coated the ground. There was no way our Expedition could have made it off the highway.

"You know what, son, we're gonna hike it! There is simply no other option," I said.

We hacked our way through, climbing over homes and trees. Helicopters appeared every now and then, searching for survivors to assist. Occasionally we'd hear a trembling voice from above—someone pleading for help after frantically climbing a tree to escape the rushing water. They carefully planted each foot on solid ground. Legs and arms shaking, covered in cuts and bruises. Clothes wet and torn. Eyes red, fighting yet another flood—this time of tears. After gathering some strength, they staggered away toward their inescapable bad news.

We reached our familiar railroad tracks, where a mountain of debris arose approximately forty-five feet high. There was no way around it. We had to climb to reach our final destination. As we scaled the wreckage, "*Kuuuuuuuurrrrrr*" constantly rang in our ears.

"What *is* that noise?" I said.

And then it hit us: It was the rush of natural gas. Before the storm, the gas hadn't been turned off within pre-existing houses, leaving a constant stream being pumped into our coastal air.

A loud racket and the shuffling of glass stole our attention. A woman was breaking into the local magic market in sheer panic. "I need milk for my baby!" she cried, holding onto her cigarette as if it were her last lifeline.

"I understand that, ma'am, but please don't smoke that cigarette. You hear that noise? That's gas! We're going to have an inferno if we're not careful!" I said.

Taking one last hit, she flattened her cigarette on the ground and continued on her way.

It took us a couple of hours to hike only three miles to our property. Unexpectedly, as we moved closer toward the water, everything cleared. No trees. No houses. Nothing. We could see all the way to the gulf. Everything was *gone*. Homes and summer escapes used to surround the beach. Beautiful oaks and pines. Now nothing remained but the ground we stood upon, with only the constant hum of gas to accompany us.

As we approached the beach, about 400 yards from where our home had resided, I gazed to my right to see our perfect, untouched road. There was nothing *anywhere*. No possessions, no people. We were the first to make it back. The location of our pier was already within view. Completely gone. Nothing remained except the pilings it stood upon. We forged ahead, though the heat of the day fought to hold us back. It was boiling *hot*—the hottest day I can remember in my *entire life*. Seagulls, beavers, pelicans, and sea otters had collapsed across the sand. Only the gradual rise and fall of their chests indicated that life remained.

Finally, our feet reunited with our property. We walked up the concrete steps leading to where our house had been less than forty-eight hours before. I sat down to take a breather, gazing out at the gulf. It was perfect. Calm, despite the occasional floating lawn mower, boat, or trailer breaking through its glass-like surface. The humidity pushed on my chest, as if the weight of Katrina on my heart wasn't enough. I had been eager to know what happened since the moment the storm lifted. Now, as I ran a finger across my forehead to direct the sweat elsewhere, I regretted getting my wish.

Apparently my goofy son knew just how to break the ice. "See if you can find the dryer, Dad, I had my clothes in it," he said with a smirk.

"Are you kidding? You left your clothes in the dryer, son!" I had to laugh. There was nothing else *to* do.

We couldn't find anything. Not a fragment of our home's structure remained. As for the cars and Harley, each were flipped and twisted, lying anywhere from forty to one hundred feet away from their original location. Our remarkable garden that I had put so much care into was destroyed. Plants that had been there twenty to thirty years, some thirty to forty feet tall—dug up from the root and vanished.

"Well, let's just catch our breath. There's nothing more we can do here," I said.

After we had absorbed as much as we could, we began our trek back to the car. The next step was to check out the restaurant. Same ordeal. I drove as far as I could, walked across the railroad tracks, and through the debris pile. We stared up and down the beach, uncovering the same thing we had at home. Only debris hung from the trees that remained. Gone. All 10,000 square feet of it. That moment will remain in my memory *forever.*

\* \* \*

After dropping Chester off safely into the hands of his mother at the emergency command center, John and I made our way back to Hattiesburg. Time inched by during our ride, despite the progress of two lanes now moving on the interstate. After a day of constant astonishment, the view continued to demand our silence. So much was destroyed, let alone the big, beautiful, concrete Bay St. Louis Bridge, which no longer existed. Around nine o'clock that night we arrived at the house. It remained powerless—completely pitch black.

Time to break the news to Starr. Absolutely nothing was left.

## A Persistent Reality

*Where are we going to go?* Only one place came to mind. So on Wednesday morning, after three days in Hattiesburg, we packed up, cleaned and secured the house, and jumped on the road to Nashville, Tennessee. Unfortunately, without electricity or cell-phone reception, we had no way to contact Ron—but I was completely out of options. We needed to take my friend up on his offer.

We arrived in Meridian, Mississippi, where only a couple of places had power. Fortunately one of them was an Applebee's. Perfect timing. Rationing frozen food that could be whipped up on the charcoal grill over the past few days didn't necessarily satisfy an appetite. Being so excited about a warm meal, we managed to forget what we would encounter inside the restaurant: the news. CNN wasn't showing updates from the gulf coast, but had full coverage of the flood in New Orleans. We watched as we ate, letting it sink in that most likely our New Orleans condo was destroyed too. Something told me there was a lot of news to come, and that very little of it would be good.

Just after crossing the Alabama state line, our phones slowly came back to life, allowing us to give Ron a tiny heads-up about his incoming houseguests. About four hours later we stumbled through Ron's front door.

"Oh my gosh! I'm so happy you are hear and safe! How about I cook dinner and we can all catch up and relax," he responded.

"I've got news for you, Ron; everything's gone. We have nowhere to go," I explained.

As could be expected, he didn't quite get it. He didn't fully understand the depth of our situation. Of course, *we* got it. We were *living* it, each and every second.

That night, Ron cooked out on the grill. We sat around the pool, drinking mass quantities of wine and sharing stories of Katrina. We simply moved through the motions of our lives that were about to drastically change. Our bodies and minds were so conflicted. *Is this real? Is our life in Waveland truly gone? But things in Nashville are so normal!* Nashville had no concept of the devastation being experienced just 500 miles south. Nobody understood. And we couldn't expect them to.

The next morning I awoke, knowing what the contents of my day held. Starr had grabbed our insurance information before leaving for Hattiesburg. So as I settled in with my morning coffee, I dialed those numbers, anticipating a strong start in what would inevitably be a marathon. Everyone around the gulf didn't even have power yet, so I was one of the first eager callers. Despite my prompt timing and thorough presentation of my policy standings, I received *nothing*. That is, nothing except one disrespectful phone call after another. Not to mention a nasty letter from our insurance company. It stated in black and white that the restaurant wasn't going to be covered, despite my federal flood insurance and windstorm pool (considered "hurricane insurance"), in addition to my regular policy. Nothing mattered. I wasn't getting a penny.

My home owner's policy played the same game. "What about my per diem? How about my money to live on? I know this is in my policy—a specific amount per day to live on for expenses for up to one year."

Finally, the woman I spoke to gave in. "Okay, we're going to give you a 2,000 dollar stipend."

Two thousand dollars. That wasn't going to get a family of four far. Because our insurance adjusters worked in states untouched by Katrina, they had no idea what we were going through or what our needs were. We were okay for the moment, but I really needed some income. I needed to do *something*. Escaping the distress seemed impossible. We didn't only lose our possessions, but our *lives* as we knew them. Internally I crumbled, knowing reality was persistently pushing us up against a hard, dead wall.

This was especially tough for Starr. After all, she had worked extremely hard alongside me for so many years, not only building our home and restaurant, but also developing a ballroom-dancing career with her partner as North American Champions. All to have it stripped away.

"What are we gonna do? Where are we going to live?" Starr managed to utter through her tears.

Though I couldn't provide her with answers, I could provide my shoulder for support. "Let it out, baby. You cry as much as you need to. Give it to me."

After a few minutes, Starr lifted her head slowly, connecting her eyes with mine. "We're going to get through this!" she declared with renewed strength.

And she was right. It was important to let out the pain. But afterward, we needed to move on.

## A New Way of Life

I couldn't do much for Ron and Louise, but at the very least I could help pay for our food to thank them. In order to do that, help was needed. I swallowed the pit in my throat as I signed my name on the food stamps application. I had never asked for anything from anybody in my entire life. However, now wasn't the time to be proud.

I created different mouth-watering dishes every night. Dinners were something to look forward to, reminding us to value what we had right then and there. We enjoyed what was left of my savory wine collection that I had spared from the storm. I'd walk out on the deck, pop open a 500 dollar bottle of wine and say with a smile, "Might as well enjoy 'em, right?"

That was how I knew we needed to live—in the moment. I needed to do things I wouldn't normally do. This was the time to enjoy life and those I loved.

## Overwhelming Kindness

About a week crawled by and being Catholic, we decided to try out Ron and Louise's church, St. Henry's. We've typically attended pretty laid-back churches, so St. Henry's, an up-scale church, was a bit of a change for us. I've always loved the warmth and friendliness of Italian priests.

"Oh, *Padre! Bon journo, Padre*," I loved saying when greeting on a Sunday.

So you can imagine my sense of ease when Father Giacosa stepped up to the pulpit to lead mass. I had never met him, but was instantly drawn to his kind nature. He was a little piece of comfort, far away from home.

"I understand a lot of people from New Orleans have come to Nashville after the devastation of Katrina. Is anyone here today a Katrina victim?" Father Giacosa asked.

With slight hesitancy, the four of us stood, followed by the whole church breaking into applause. We absorbed the support, not quite sure what we had done to deserve this reception, but appreciating it all the same. When mass ended, Father made a point of coming over to say hello, offering his assistance with anything we needed.

\* \* \*

Meanwhile, our children were doing their best to cope—Laura being too strong for her own good, while John attempted to let go of everything he knew back in Waveland. John was in his second year of college at the University of South Alabama, which was pretty much untouched by the storm. However, Laura's high-school in Mississippi, Our Lady Academy, had been completely destroyed. So Starr and I wracked our brains for ideas regarding Laura's schooling. She needed a place to belong again.

Ron and Louise's daughters had attended a grammar school called Overbrook, sharing a campus with St. Cecilia Academy, a prestigious all-girl's high school. This became our starting point. Sitting down with Sister Mary Thomas, Starr and Laura explained our story and inquired about probable options.

"She starts tomorrow. We'll waive tuition, don't you worry about it," Sister Mary said as she extended her arms out to us, holding a uniform and textbooks.

Our hearts leapt with joy and relief. *Did that just really happen? This was a big deal!* We had a school for our daughter. Suddenly,

Nashville looked a bit different. Maybe we could call it home for a while? Either way, we were eternally grateful for Sister Mary Thomas' overwhelming kindness.

> **"When life gets too hard to stand, kneel."**
> ~Gordon B. Hinckley

* * *

Father Giacosa could see the distress draped across my face week after week at church. "Hang in there," he'd say to me.

Three words—that was it. And yet there was more truth in those words than I knew. "You can't do anything about what has happened. Whatever you do, don't give up. Hang in there. Things will clear."

So that's what I did, short of dropping to my knees each week and doing some *serious* praying for strength. That's what I would ask God for. Not materials or a job, but for strength to make it through.

> **"So do not fear, for I am with you; do not be dismayed,**
> **for I am your God. I will strengthen you and help you;**
> **I will uphold you with my righteous right hand."**
> Isaiah 41:10
> (NIV)

I had nothing going on at that time in terms of work, though providing for my family was never far from my mind. One Sunday, Father Giacosa approached me.

"Ohhh, my goodness! I hear you were a chef with your own restaurant down on the coast. We sure could use some good food here in Nashville, you know."

I hadn't even considered that. There were so many unknowns to deliberate. But despite my uncertainties, Father Giacosa planted a small seed that day, whether either of us knew it or not.

## Rumors

September and October came and went while I struggled to lead my family. I wouldn't let them watch a lot of news. The details were so depressing—nothing but destruction, flood water, and the politics of FEMA. Those who had lost their homes to Katrina were in so much trouble—hotels kicking them out, having nowhere to go. We would watch about ten minutes to catch the important updates and then shut it off. News alerts constantly forced in your face may provide awareness, but their weight will also hold you down.

Constant rumors were circulating, really freaking us out. Stories of friends and people we knew who had died, found lying on the beach. At the time, it was impossible to know if these accounts held truth or if bodies had been misidentified. Our cell phone company had been destroyed in the storm, leaving us with second-hand communication at best. Once we were able to find a new company, I finally had a phone in hand, calling as many sources as I could—at least those with phones.

I hung up and said to Starr, "We are really lucky not to be sitting in that debris. In an odd way, God has brought us to Nashville. I don't know why, but we could easily be stuck back home in the drive-through of Hancock Bank, trying to make a house out of the remaining overhang like some of our friends."

Nothing made sense at the time, but we knew we still had a great deal to be thankful for.

## Claim Mania

We continued to work on our many claims, hoping to receive some type of compensation. I was assigned to Darrell*, my Insurance Claims Adjuster in Boulder, CO. When I inquired once again about the status of my claim, Darrell spouted out in anger, "You know, I could delay this claim for six more months if I wanted to! I don't have to deal with this right now."

"Why are you being this way to me? I've paid my premium for twenty-five years. I'm just asking for my policy limits. Why won't you just pay my claim?" I responded.

But his hot-headed response never changed.

> **"Be kinder than necessary, for everyone you meet is fighting some kind of battle."**
> ~*T.H. Thompson and John Watson*

We tried to stay focused, telling ourselves that our situation would get better, despite the dense cloud of doubt that loomed over our heads. Hearing my constant frustration, followed by zero progress, Louise jumped in, using her experience as an attorney to help write letters to our insurance company. Her selective use of legal terms drew attention to the company's refusal to work for their customer. Approximately two weeks later, a certified letter was in our hands requesting additional time.

Finally, my auto-insurance company offered approximately 25,000 dollars for my Corvette, Mustang, and Harley combined. They were all in my garage during the storm, therefore, supported by my home-owner's policy.

"You know, this is highway robbery," I said to my agent. "The Corvette and the Mustang were both showroom cars, in pristine condition."

But I hung my head, knowing I had to accept what they were offering, despite the brutal mistreatment. I was really low on funds and needed some breathing room. Our bank in Mississippi had been destroyed, leaving me unable to locate my banker. But of course, God had a plan that I couldn't have seen ahead of time. Thankfully, I had a few thousand dollars saved in another bank that ironically had survived Katrina. You don't realize why life plays out as it does until you look back after the storm.

## Independence on Percy Warner

Toward the end of October, our federal flood insurance kicked in, issuing us a lump sum of money.

"Halleluiah!" I shouted as my nerves unwound for the first time in months.

I certainly hadn't received the amount that we were entitled through our policies, but this was at least part of it. A big, *big* break.

"Oh man, this is good! We're going to be able to move ahead," I said to Starr.

It was definitely a priority to move out of Ron and Louise's house. Starr and I traveled around Nashville looking for places that were within our budget. Finally we found a great house—about 1,500 square feet. Three small bedrooms, two baths, nice yard, good area—right by St. Henry's.

"Well, we know where we go to church! Can't beat the location," I said.

The house was simple but very inviting, complete with hardwood floors and lots of charm. However, I was in for a blow that would put my feet back on the ground: 250,000 dollars! The same house would only be 100,000 dollars back in Waveland.

We knew a good find when we saw one, so we took the leap and put an offer down. But no surprise here ... I couldn't get financed. I didn't even have a job. I of course had the money for the down payment, with more money sure to come in from my claims. But in the meantime, I needed some help. Not a lot of friends would let you live in their house for two months, let alone what was about to happen. Ron drove to the bank, got the loan in his name, and secured it under his credit (using my money for the down payment). And it worked! We were in! All thanks to Ron.

We closed on a Thursday, finally independent again in our little house on Percy Warner. On Sunday afternoon I decided to make something tasty for our new neighbors. They were bound to meet us sooner or later so why not introduce ourselves with a killer gallon of gumbo! Sunset rolled in as we walked to our next door neighbor's house.

"Hi, we're the Chapmans and we just moved in. I made some gumbo and thought we'd get to know you by bringing some over. We're from New Orleans."

They smiled graciously. "That's so sweet! But well, we're vegetarians ... and we're Jewish."

"Well, you just want the rice?" I asked once our laughter subsided.

Next stop was the guy across the little creek. What were the odds? He turned out to be a vegetarian too! What was going on? This was *some* town! But at least he took the gumbo.

"I'm gonna eat it on the side and not tell my wife," he admitted.

Starr and I laughed yet again as we continued on our way, crossing the street on the right side of our house.

A guy opened the door and said, "Hi! Nice to meet you. I'm Jim Morrison."

"What? I thought you were *dead!*" I exclaimed, enjoying yet another round of laughs with our new neighbor. "We brought you some homemade gumbo!"

"Ooohhhh, I *love* gumbo!" he shouted, eyes wide with excitement. *Thank God—a real person!*

And *that's* how we met our neighbors. But adjusting to this new home was difficult. Our surroundings were very different, living in a community instead of on the beach; sharing 1,500 square feet as opposed to 7,000 surrounded by four acres; not having any of our old possessions—not with concern for their worth, but for their memories. We had a spectacular life in Waveland. A life that existed only in our minds now, and those who understood were far away. But most importantly, we were happy. We were doing okay.

> **"The greatest thing in this world is not so much where we are, but in what direction we are moving."**
> ~Oliver Wendell Holmes, Jr.

## Life on the Corner of Church Street

We had now been in our new house about a week. Where was I going to work? Three months had passed since we'd arrived in Nashville. Not one to sit on my butt, I needed to get moving. We toyed around with a bunch of different options, though nothing was a good fit. I didn't want to uproot my family again, or take ten steps back in my career.

In search of inspiration, Ron and I drove around town, keeping our eyes peeled for the slightest hint of opportunity.

"You know, how about here in Nashville? Why don't we just open a little place?" I said.

Pulling up to 18th and Church Street, we noticed a big sign on the corner building that read: *For Sale/For Lease – Nick Spiva.*

"Hey, that's a pretty cool corner. I kinda like it!" I announced. We got out of the car and checked out the building while I called the number on the sign.

After explaining who I was and my possible intentions for the space, Nick drove down from his office in Green Hills to meet us. He described the basics of the lease and handed me the keys.

"Go in. Call me later. Let me know what you think," Nick said.

And he was gone. Ron and I walked through the space, checking out every inch. It was a *big* place, but Nick wasn't asking for a lot to lease it.

"Man, Ron, this is pretty good for the money. I'd have to renovate the whole thing, but with my claims coming in, I could do it. If I kept my overhead down it just might work out."

My excitement picked up speed as the words fell from my mouth.

"Nick, I'm really interested," I said when I called him that evening.

"You just work it out. Keep the keys for a couple days. Get a contractor in there. Don't worry, I'm not going to rent it to anybody else. If you want it, it's yours."

Ron recommended a contractor who had worked on his house. We brought him in the next day, explained my objectives, and received a quote. I knew a lot of construction and subcontractor surprises were in my future, but most importantly, the sum was manageable, and at the time I just wanted it to work so badly. The destruction after Katrina was so substantial, I couldn't see waiting for the restoration in order to rebuild in that area. I needed to do something in that moment. And there it stood, this building on Church Street, begging for some life.

Before I could change my mind, I quickly dialed Nick's number. "I think we wanna do it!"

"Deal. Don't even worry about the rent. It's yours. If you get all the work done on the building in three months and you're in, we can do rent that first month you open. But if you open before the three months then you'll start paying rent on that day."

"That sounds great, Nick. That's very fair, and I appreciate it."

I couldn't wait to tell Father Giacosa! The Sunday after I sealed the deal, I said to him, "Guess what, Father! I just leased a restaurant."

With a broad smile he exclaimed, "Well, alllright! Looking forward to eating some good gumbo! Can't wait for you to open!"

But he didn't have to wait long. Grinning from ear to ear, I swiftly placed a gallon of my fresh gumbo in the hands of one of my biggest supporters.

That's how *Chappy's on Church* came to life. We signed the lease on December 1, 2005. Nine months after Katrina, on June 13, 2006, we were open for business, bringing the experience of charm, comfort, love, and life that *is* New Orleans.

## A Purpose

I'll never regret anything I've done in my life, though many times I've pondered, "The Road Not Taken." *What if I would have just rented a house in Nashville and waited for things to have gotten a little better on the coast?* We missed witnessing the recovery. We missed people returning for the first time after the storm—frequent diners who grew into dear friends.

No arm of government could have done anything more than what had been done. Rescue teams couldn't even get into the area, let alone save the day. FEMA did what they could, as they always had.

Sometimes in the politics of it all, the truth gets twisted, laying blame. But the truth is, there's just nothing anyone could do. However, that didn't stop me from inventing the FEMA Martini—"'cause it takes a while to hit'cha!" After all, if you can't joke about it, what *can* you do?

We later learned that our one surviving possession was our New Orleans condo. However, this journey had never been about material goods. We lost our *lives*. Our lifestyle. Our church and school. Our neighbors. *Everything.* I held on to Father Giacosa's advice to hang in there, kept praying, and kept moving forward. It may sound simplistic, but sometimes, when the road behind you is gone, you only have the steps in front of you to focus on. The storm and loss were our history. And if Katrina taught me anything, it was that we had to live life for today because tomorrow could be *gone*.

## We Can Get Up

Living my entire life in hurricane alley, I witnessed some of the most aggressive storms. But I can honestly say they've been nothing like Katrina. We had this storm … so big … so powerful … such a catastrophe. I hope we never see another like it. People tend to fear history, thinking that the past will come back and bite them once again. And quite honestly, it might. But we can't fear it. We would never enjoy the here and now. Eliminate the worry for tomorrow— but always *hope* for a better one.

> **"If you spend your whole life waiting for the storm, you'll never enjoy the sunshine."**
> ~Morris West

Easy answers weren't realistic, and no one else was going to do the work for me. I had to search for answers on my own. And to others who are on a similar search, just know that you *can* make it through, no matter what happens. Pick yourself up, dust yourself off, and go back at it. Look at yourself in the mirror and say, "I can do

this. I can get up." We are only as good as what we can make from
our experiences.

> **"We also have joy with our troubles, because we know**
> **that these troubles produce patience. And patience**
> **produces character, and character produces hope."**
> Romans 5:3-4
> (NCV)

I could never fully describe the depth of our difficulties. It was
brutal for everyone Katrina affected. We just did the best we could,
trying not to look back. God created us for a reason, not to sit here
and deteriorate. Things happen, no doubt about it. But good things
happen too.

> **"Although the world is full of suffering, it**
> **is full also of the overcoming of it."**
> ~Helen Keller

People always ask me, "Didn't you take photographs of the
destruction?"

I always say, "Absolutely not! Why would I take photographs of
the destruction? I want to remember the good times. The way it was."

So that's it. Here I am. Enjoying the good times.

*Names or locations have been changed to protect those involved.

Reflection Questions

1. During the recession in 1983, Chappy made the decision to change career paths. How did his past experiences prepare him for an unexpected career in the restaurant business? Do life experiences yield drastic turning-points or does each minuscule turn present valuable stepping stones?

2. Is it easy to maintain the balance between living for today and planning for the future? What actions can be taken in order to maintain this type of outlook?

3. Chappy didn't have any regrets, but he does admit to occasionally letting his mind wander down "the road not taken." Is it ever too late to take a different road? Is there a new direction in your life that has been requesting your faith?

4. Our lives are constantly changing. The sun's rays will break through the clouds after a storm, but that doesn't assure us that high winds and rain aren't in our future once again. Upon experiencing and recovering from a significant calamity, are we ever assured a happy-ever-after? More importantly, should that be the goal? Or should the goal be the strength of our focus within the struggle itself?

# The Perpetual Spark: Seeds of Growth

## Enjoy life.

After faced with the devastation of Katrina, Chappy knew it was time to roll up his sleeves in search of his next steps. As much as we dread facing our challenges, there is nothing like the sense of accomplishment upon reaching the other side. However, if we're not careful, our efforts to overcome and succeed can become our main objectives, suffocating the need to enjoy life itself.

Ultimately, we were not blessed with life so that we could whittle away at our never-ending to-do lists. The accomplishment from a productive day can be satisfying. However, constant agenda items can distract us from what's important. After all, what's so great about crossing off a task from the list if the only reward is jotting down another?

We all have a very real need for balance, a fine line that we walk allowing us to be productive, but also to give ourselves a break and enjoy today. If the success of our day is determined by one focus alone, other areas of our lives will no doubt suffer. Distributing time fairly between productivity, relaxation, and quality time with God, family, and friends eliminates the deficit. We become positive, energized, and fulfilled versions of ourselves. Chappy did just that. His days were plagued with claim deliberation and stress, while his evenings focused on creating exceptional moments with those he loved.

> **"One hand full of rest is better than two fists**
> **full of labor and striving after wind."**
> *Ecclesiastes 4:6*
> *(NASB)*

*Do* enjoy life. Work hard and with passion. But also remember to charge your battery. Play hooky once in a while from your structured calendar. Make yourself a priority. Grab a cup of coffee with a dear friend. Watch a good movie. Dive head first into a sport. Reconnect with our Creator. Order a decadent dessert before your entree. Call a family member to catch up. Do something new and exciting that you've always dreamed of doing. Lose yourself in a book. Take a day off just because. Set aside time to just ... *be.*

Enjoy today, it's the only one you have.

# CHAPTER 6

## Kathy's Story ~ The Watchman

**"I love you and I would never leave you. During your times of suffering, when you could see only one set of footprints, it was then that I carried you."**
~Footprints in the Sand, Poem; Author Unknown

omewhere between 11.00-11.30 p.m. the phone rang. It was my brother-in-law Mike. He had been at our house the day before for a barbecue when he and my husband Tim had initially discussed going to the Tigers game in downtown Detroit. "Is Tim home yet?" he asked, having already returned home from the game.

"No, not yet," I replied.

"How was your night, Kathy?" I heard my sister say after stealing the phone from Mike.

But my answer was short-lived. Another voice was on the line … and it wasn't a family member's.

The operator had intercepted our call, stating she was connecting me to an emergency call with the Wayne County Medical Board. I had no idea what was happening, but it was happening at lightning speed.

"Hello, ma'am. Does a man named Tim Parish live at your residence?" a man asked.

"Yes. Oh my God, what's wrong? Do I have to come to the hospital? Did something happen?"

A flash of silence passed before he continued. "Well, ma'am, I'm very sorry to tell you this, but we believe that your husband has been killed near Tiger Stadium."

> **"I guess we're all one phone call from our knees."**
> ~Mat Kearney

## The Beginning

I met Tim in my senior year of high school. In the middle of class, he leaned over and asked, "What's your name?"

My signature on my homework assignment must have caught his eye.

"Kathy Morrill," I responded, curious as to his sudden interest.

"Are you Sergeant Morrill's daughter?"

"Yes. Why, do you know him?"

"Yeah," he responded reluctantly, explaining how they had met. My father was a police officer for the St. Clair Shores Police Department. Tim apparently had gotten into trouble after deciding to steal a case of beer off of a truck parked outside a party store. Ironically, Dad was the officer who had arrested him—not the best first impression. When the time came, Tim was very nervous to "meet" Dad for the second time.

I came home from school ready to initiate the conversation.

"Dad, this guy is coming over today so that we can work on some homework together. But ... you know him. His name is Tim." I cautiously reminded Dad of their unfortunate first encounter. My body tensed, absorbing the silence.

"Well ... that's okay, as long as he's straightened up now."

I giggled in relief, picturing Tim's face as he arrived at my house.

Who knew that these awkward moments were the start of something big? Tim and I married on November 26, 1972, about five years after we graduated from high school.

## Curve Ball

After our wedding, Tim and I were completely in sync. Each day I awoke, eager to spend it with my best friend. But then I started to notice changes in Tim. He was rarely home. And when he was, he was distant and moody. None of this made sense, until the truth came to light: Tim was having an affair. My insides tore. This couldn't be true! Despite that Tim was occasionally seeing another woman, he made it clear that he didn't want a divorce. But if that were truly the case, why would he continue being unfaithful? I knew Tim loved me, but he was acting as if this was a game, and I was his collateral.

*Why would he stray?* That question ran through my head constantly. I loved him so much and thought I was showing him that. Tim wanted to have his sweet, picturesque family—his wife at home, taking care of our son Timmy. But He also wanted the freedom to go out and party with his friends. His core values had taken the back seat. It was as if he were being manipulated. The devil found a weakness and walked through that open door.

\* \* \*

Most believers *develop* a faith in God. I was different. For as long as I can remember—from day one—I have *always* believed in God. I have never known or wanted to know a life without Him. However, I never realized the personal relationship we could share. During the turmoil swirling around my marriage to Tim, a friend invited me to go to church with her. I accepted the invitation, eager to receive any help I could find.

Oddly enough, the sermon included a true story about a woman who had also struggled with her husband's infidelity. She made it her mission to show her husband how much she loved him and that she was dedicated to making the marriage work. Every day before her husband left the house, no matter where he was going, she'd prepare his clothes, placing them on the bed. She did anything she could think of to show her love, support, and belief in their marriage. Then every

Sunday she'd return to church to receive support and guidance. Her husband couldn't watch her do this anymore! He finally recognized whatever the Lord wanted him to see through her actions. That man gave his heart to God and in turn, healed their marriage.

Could God have planned that message specifically for me? Hunched-over in the church pew, I sobbed uncontrollably. I just couldn't believe that this was my reality! Yet, I discovered something that I *could* believe: God could heal our marriage. If this woman could do it, maybe so could I.

From that moment forward, everything I did was with the intent of being a supportive wife. I prayed every single day that Tim would realize what we had was too valuable to treat with such disrespect. His friends provided me with updates, but the most recent was alarming.

"Tim is trying to pull away from her, Kathy. But she's very persistent; she refuses to loosen her grip," I was told.

But that didn't stop Tim's resistance. He made it clear that he was ready to make changes, *big* changes. He was staying home more, wanting to spend more quality time with me and the boys. He was more attentive and caring, often professing how much he loved us. Though Tim didn't share my faith in God, our relationship slowly improved. During the following year and a half, I continued to go the extra mile to show how much I loved him. I wasn't giving up, not by a long shot.

In early June, we took off for the Budweiser Boat Races in Detroit. The sun pressed upon us while we eagerly walked toward the event hand-in-hand. As we approached the water, the hint of diesel fuel surprised my nose. Hearing the engines rev with anticipation, we knew things were about to get exciting! We sat with friends, watching the thick spray of water trail the boats as they sped past. Tim was never far from me, checking to see if I were hungry or in need of a cold drink. For the first time in a long time, we were so connected. As we strolled back to the car, Tim slipped his arm around my back and squeezed me gently. God was at work. I could feel it.

The night came to an end with a confession from Tim: "I love you so much, Kathy. Please always remember that."

And in my heart I knew ... everything was going to be okay.

## Boys Night Out

On the scorching-hot day of July 2, Tim came home from work, greeting his family with a smile. By this time, our son, Timmy, was two years old. We also had recently received another precious blessing: our newborn son, Tristan, who was a mere thirteen weeks. I couldn't have been happier! Not only was our marriage healing, but we had two beautiful kids.

The prior weekend, Tim had put together a swing-set as Timmy's third birthday present, in preparation for his upcoming party on July 5. Timmy idolized his dad, always glued to his side, mimicking Tim's actions to a tee. And believe me, the feeling was mutual. Tim's eyes lit up when he saw his boys.

But that night was baseball night. Tim had been looking forward to going to a Detroit Tigers game that evening with his good friend Mark and brother-in-law Mike. My husband worked extremely hard, definitely deserving a night out with the guys. Tim and Mark did pretty much everything together, which not only included watching baseball, but playing in a league as well.

Before leaving, Tim picked up Timmy and held him with one arm. With his other arm wrapped around me, he kissed us one after the other. "I love my little family so much. Be good tonight, okay?"

He then walked over to Tristan, lying comfortably in his crib. While patting him on his little bottom, Tim gave Tristan a gentle kiss good-bye.

Tim left that night for Tiger Stadium, never to return home again.

## The Smile

My body became like ice.

"Are you all right, ma'am?" he asked.

"No, I'm not all right!" I hung up and called my sister and Mike back, my fingers shaking uncontrollably.

I fell to my knees, crying, desperately begging, "Oh Lord, please don't let it be Tim! Maybe someone stole his wallet and they have the wrong ID? *Please* don't let it be Tim!"

The next thing I knew, Mark and my family were by my side. I had absolutely no idea what to do with myself; I was in such a deep state of shock.

The next day, Tim's brother, Jeff, identified the body. I just couldn't bring myself to do it. "How did he look?" I asked, not sure if I wanted to know the answer.

"He had a smile on his face, Kathy," Jeff replied.

Oh Lord, how could he have been smiling after the way he had been killed? Tim had been ruthlessly stabbed several times. Witnesses reported seeing two men fighting. One fell to the ground but quickly jumped back up, running after the victim as he tried to escape (assumed to be Tim). Arms flailed through the air toward the victim, upon which one of the witnesses screamed out, "He's had enough, stop it!"

My husband's life was taken because another man saw the opportunity to steal his possessions. Tim wouldn't have let anyone rob him without putting up a fight. Yet, he had a *smile* on his face? How could that *be*? The rest remained a mystery.

## Good-Byes and Decisions

Should Timmy come to the funeral home to see his father? I wrestled with this question constantly, not knowing how to handle the situation.

"What do you think I should do? Do people often bring their young children into situations like this?" I asked the funeral-home attendants.

"We know that's a tough decision, Kathy. However, it most likely won't matter either way. It's highly unlikely that Timmy will remember going anyway."

Desperately hoping they were right, I decided not to take him.

Many people came to the funeral home to pay their respects. Tim was only twenty-nine years old. You just couldn't help but love him; he would give anyone the shirt off his back. As a result, he had a lot of friends. They walked up to me, one by one, unable to speak. I couldn't blame them in the least. Yet surprisingly, I didn't cry or fall apart. The strength that I displayed was not my own.

Before the minister gave the eulogy, he pulled me aside. "Kathy, I truly believe that at the time Tim was attacked, there had been a spiritual battle going on between Satan and Jesus. Satan was trying to claim Tim, just as the Bible states that he comes to steal, kill, and destroy."

> **"The thief comes only to steal and kill and destroy.**
> **I came that they may have life and have it abundantly."**
> John 10:10
> (ESV)

I was thankful for him sharing this with me, but it was a lot to swallow. I needed more time. I needed to get through the day. One step at a time. *God, continue to hold me up.*

The moment came for the final good-bye. As I approached the casket, an unexpected item captured my attention. A bumper sticker lay next to Tim that read: *Honk if you love Willie Nelson.* A small smile crept across my face. Tim loved Willie Nelson. He bought concert tickets every chance he could.

Just before the casket closed, I peeled the sticker off the white backing, securing it across Tim's chest. Without fail, every time I passed the cemetery I made sure to honk my horn. He would get a big kick out of that.

\* \* \*

Not until after the funeral did I realize the mistake I had made. Timmy should have gone to the funeral home to see his father one last time—the man who was in his life one day, and without warning, gone from reach the next. I struggled to let go of my regret for that decision—a decision that I've had to live with every day since.

But there was one mistake I wasn't going to make—I *would* follow through and give Timmy a birthday party on July 5 as we had planned. It was beyond difficult, but I was not about to let him down. After everyone left, Timmy and I sat down at the wooden picnic table in the backyard. A day that typically ends with smiles and testing out new toys, instead concluded with every part of Timmy's face falling toward the ground. Though my heart resisted, I knew this was the moment.

"Timmy, I want to talk to you about something. You probably wonder where your father has been."

"Yes. I miss him, Momma," he said, his eyebrows drawing together.

"I miss him too, sweetheart, *so* much. I want you to know, though, that Jesus had to come and get your daddy. Daddy's in heaven, but he can't come back home again. He's happy there and he's watching over you! He loves you, me, and Tristan. Someday we will see Daddy again."

He rested his little head on the table, not saying anything for a few minutes. Then slowly he whispered, "Momma, I want Jesus to drive my daddy back home."

It broke my heart.

Fear surged through me. Every part of me tensed in anticipation of the life that was still to come. I couldn't even take care of myself, let alone my children! How could people be outside, driving around, and going about their days? Didn't they know that my world had just stopped? My husband was gone! I couldn't believe others were still functioning because I most definitely was just getting by.

> **"If fear is cultivated it will become stronger, if faith is cultivated it will achieve mastery."**
> ~John Paul Jones

## Unanswered Questions

"Satan was trying to claim Tim ...."

I couldn't get the minister's words out of my head, although this perspective didn't come as a complete surprise.

Approximately three months before his attack, Tim brought his friend Todd* home from work. A surprising subject surfaced between the three of us. Sadly, Todd had been beaten by his father throughout his childhood.

"If there is a God, how could He let such *horrible* things happen to good people?" he asked.

Though I tried to provide some clarity and support, I knew full well that some answers only God can provide. But as the conversation came to an end, something inside told me what I needed to say next.

"Well, I just want to tell both of you that if you are ever close to death, call upon the Lord Jesus. Call out for Jesus and you can be forgiven of your sins."

I'm not sure where the words came from, I just knew they had to be said.

\* \* \*

Throughout our marriage and my concern for Tim's salvation, I prayed tirelessly for a spark of faith to ignite within him. In the meantime, I held on to these words with all of my might:

> **"They replied, 'Believe in the Lord Jesus, and you will be saved—you and your household.'"**
> *Acts 16:31*
> *(NIV)*

One night while Tim was out, I lowered my hands and knees to the familiar cushion of my brown, shag, bedroom carpet as I had done countless times before. "Lord, I don't care what it takes for Tim's salvation, I'll go through it."

At that very moment, the thought of death swept through my mind. *What? Did I just imagine that? Tim would have to* die? In shock, I responded, "Oh no, Lord, not in that way!"

I had no idea why that thought was put into my head or if it held any truth. However, approximately one month after that moment Tim was taken from me. Why did it have to be this way! Couldn't there have been another road? Regardless of my questions, I realized that I had to hang on to my faith. It was the only thing that would save me.

## He Was There

After about three months had passed, reality set in. I loved my husband so deeply. To say that I was "devastated" would be an understatement. He was everything to me. My heart physically ached, preventing my lungs from finding their gentle rhythm. *Who am I without him?* I had no idea. *I'll never be that same person again.* I lived one day at a time, but the pain of each minute felt as if it would last forever.

Despite my faith, I was extremely angry. God had let me down! I had prayed for so long, fighting for Tim with every part of me. Our marriage had been healing! We were going to be okay! Now, not only did I have to recover from the pain of Tim's infidelity, but I also had to deal with losing him completely.

The boys had just gone down for their nap as I forced my legs toward the basement steps. I couldn't avoid it forever. Hunched over Tim's mound of dirty clothes, I began sorting each piece as the silence closed in around me. Their texture, their smell—every detail carried a memory, with the reminder that memories were all I had left. I cried out, "Lord, why did this have to happen? I *trusted* in You! I trusted in You for my husband's salvation! I prayed and prayed for *years*, truly believing that it was going to happen. But why did it have to happen like *this*?"

Silence. That was always what followed. That was the toughest part, not receiving the answers that I so desperately needed. I was utterly lost. But despite my anger and confusion, I continued to pray, day in and day out. Somewhere in the midst, the minister's words surfaced yet again, "... a spiritual battle had been going on between Satan and Jesus. Satan was trying to claim Tim ...."

God hadn't caused this—it was truly the devil. While that eased my anger, it did nothing for the pain.

* * *

My emotional struggle was relentless, as was the endless list of items on my to-do list. Parenting with two parents is hard enough, let alone reduced to only one. One exhausting day in October, I begged God to show me His presence. Leaves had been falling by the truckloads across every square inch of our yard. I was so emotionally and physically drained, in no way could I find the energy to rake my entire lawn on top of everything else I had to do. I cried to God in desperation.

"Lord, You know how You said You'd be the husband to the widow and a father to our children? How am I supposed to get out there and rake all my leaves? I have these two little children and I just can't do it."

The next morning I staggered toward the window, ready to glare at what plagued me. *But how ... ? You have got to be kidding!* Not one leaf lay on my front lawn! Ours was the only property on the street whose grass was completely leaf-free. A trickle of laughter leapt from my mouth, followed by the faintest sigh of relief. *You know, You really do care about me and my children.* It wasn't the greatest day in the world for my neighbors, but deep down I knew God had provided for us, and that He wasn't going anywhere.

* * *

The days were long, but at times, the nights even longer. My pillow took a beating as I tossed and turned, desperate for some sleep to relieve my exhaustion. I finally managed to drift off, though this illusion of rest didn't last long. I awoke sensing a deep stillness—a quiet peace covering the room like the ocean's tide over sand.

"Kathy, I hear you."

For a moment, my breathing ceased. The air was so calm, filled only with that voice. A voice I had never heard. I knew it was the Lord. Such a beautiful voice.

> **"Peace is not the absence of conflict, but the presence of God no matter what the conflict."**
> *~Anonymous*

But this wasn't an isolated incident. Another night I was woken by a brilliant light blazing from the corner of my bedroom. A figure stood within its glow, appearing to be a shepherd, grasping a shepherd's stick. It couldn't have been anyone *but* Jesus, although due to the light's radiance I couldn't see His face. I stared, frozen in disbelief. Was I dreaming or was this real? I turned over to wake a friend who was staying the night, eager to show her what I was seeing! But the second I looked back, the room returned to darkness.

> **"I am the good shepherd; I know my sheep and my sheep know me—"**
> *John 10:14*
> *(NIV)*

The Lord came to me that night. He came to say, "Kathy, I am your shepherd. I am watching over you and your children. I know your pain. And I am here for you."

I fell asleep with such peace. He really *did* know me, and we were in His hands.

> **"Every evening I turn my worries over to God. He's going to be up all night anyway."**
> *~Mary C. Crowley*

* * *

These moments brought me closer to God in a way that I didn't know was possible. As hard as I tried to take care of myself and my family, I was constantly reminded that I had to rely on Him for everything.

## My Inner Shell

I had no idea what we were going to do for Christmas, our first Christmas without Tim. I had heard that after losing someone, you should do something totally out of the ordinary—something you've never done. My in-laws lived in Tampa, Florida, so I decided we would spend Christmas with them. They were also still deeply grieving, so they were excited I was coming to liven things up with the boys.

As I had feared, the holidays were excruciating, so I decided to distract myself with a walk down the beach. I needed some time to think and regroup. The beach was completely bare—no shells, no rocks. As I shuffled my feet through the sand, I somehow stumbled across this shell … this one beautiful shell that came out of nowhere. I loved shells, so I saved it and brought it home to show my sister and friends. This was a small moment—a small treasure—but I knew to hold onto all of the good moments that came my way.

After the trip ended, despite appreciating our time with my in-laws, I still couldn't find my footing. Little did I know, the deep end of my pool was about to get deeper. In January, I received a call from the detective working on Tim's case.

"This may be it, Kathy. We have a man in our custody that we believe to be Tim's attacker."

My teeth clenched as I glared at his picture printed in the newspaper. This could be the man with whom Tim fought for his life.

It was bad enough to see him in the paper, let alone attend the trial in February. I had no idea how I'd get through it, but I had to be there. As far as I was concerned, that courtroom could have been the

Alicia M. Smith

size of a football field, and yet, wouldn't have been big enough. It was uncovered that this man had been staying at a half-way house at night while installing roofs during the day. He had been hurt on a roofing job before Tim's attack, supporting the eye-witness' statement that the attacker had been limping as he ran from the scene.

In the end, there wasn't enough evidence to convict. The man on trial was released. But that didn't change what my gut was screaming: They had caught the right man. I was informed later that supposedly, Tim's alleged killer had given his heart to God. However, that didn't matter to me—his belief couldn't bring my boys' father back. My heart had hardened. The damage had been done.

\* \* \*

The winter months dragged on. Pain continued to hover over me—around me—through me. I stumbled through my routines, searching for any amount of normalcy. My mother and aunt must have known that I needed a change of pace when they approached me about returning to Florida for a little vacation. When we arrived, the memory of that Christmas shell popped into my head. Wanting to connect with God again, I prayed that I would find another shell, a special one from Him. I needed to feel Him again. I needed the reassurance that only God could provide.

Because it was Easter season, the beaches were extremely crowded. However, I wasn't going to let that stop me. The three of us managed to make it down to the water while my mother-in-law watched the boys at home. As we walked, I couldn't help but scour the sand for another shell. But nothing spectacular caught my eye. Every single one appeared identical to the one before. Eventually, my aunt and I landed upon a secluded area down the beach.

"Would you like this shell?" a voice behind me said.

I was slightly distracted, still dedicated to my hunt.

"Kathy," Aunt Jenn said, "this woman wants to know if you want this shell."

My excitement rose as I focused on the conch shell, about three inches in length. The outside was plain but shiny, reflecting the sun's rays toward me. However, the inside was filled with gorgeous color. As I held it up to the light, it appeared to have an image shining through an opening on one side, directly toward the opposite solid wall. It was so unlike anything I'd ever seen.

I was so grateful, eager to thank the three people standing before us. I tried to focus on them, but the sun's light shown directly on their faces, preventing me from seeing their features clearly.

"Thank you so very much! I really appreciate this," I said as the women handed me the shell.

My face beamed as I looked over at my aunt. I quickly turned back to watch them walk away, my gaze combing the beach from one side to the other. I couldn't see them anywhere!

"Did you see their faces, Aunt Jenn? Who were they?" I said, stunned by their disappearance.

"No, Kathy, I couldn't see their faces. It was so strange!"

Those three people that day were my angels. God was right next to me. He showed me that, time and time again. Knowing this, my lonely moments weren't as lonely. Sleep became less rare—a weight had been lifted—we had someone else to watch over us. And Tim wasn't the only one who could love me. God had enough love to cover our entire family. Whatever I needed, He was there.

### Humor in Unlikely Places

God has a sense of humor. It's not every day that a person gets to experience it, but I was getting to know Him on a different level.

"How about we take the boys to Big Boy for dinner, Kathy?" my sister Pam suggested.

I loved being with my sister—she is such an inspiration, having strong faith in God while always giving off that spark that shines in any setting. Pam often helped with the boys and did whatever she could to keep my spirits up.

On the ride home, we somehow drifted into a conversation about heaven and having faith. Blind faith can be hard to understand. I tried to explain how I still maintained my faith, even after all that I had been through. I couldn't seem to find the right words to communicate my thoughts, so I just laughed and said, "You know what, Pam, you just know what you know. You *know* what you *know*."

I didn't know how else to say it! Sometimes there's just no other way to describe it other than, "You just know." Without a doubt, that truly is the definition of faith.

As we approached a stop-light, a bumper sticker caught my eye on the car in front of us. It read: "I know that you know what you know." Laughter filled the car as my eyes trailed toward the night's sky. Once again, God reassured my faith, and in a very unexpected way.

\* \* \*

After about a year had passed, my days had gotten a little easier. But regardless, I was still angry. *Why did this have to happen? There had to have been something I could have done!* Round and round I went on the grief cycle's merry-go-round. I couldn't escape. But life wouldn't just get better on its own. I had to take control. So I made the decision to go to counseling. Every day I worked at letting go. Letting go of the anger. Letting go of the questions. Letting go of my habit of going through life's motions, taking my moments for granted.

> **"Have the life you want by being fully present to the life you have."**
> ~Mark Nepo

However, the boys knew just how to snap me out of it. One evening, without warning, Tristan and Timmy discovered the cooking oil in the kitchen cupboard. Before I knew it, Tristan was slipping and sliding all over the place.

"Oh no, not the brand new carpet!" I shouted in desperation.

Too late. Timmy decided it was time to take a stroll!

But wait! What was that God-awful smell? Oh yes, a diaper surprise wafted from Tristan, leaving me ready to break down at any second. Instead, I released a burst of laughter, knowing I had to surrender to the craziness. There was no controlling the chaos even if I wanted to. The boys truly kept me going in a way no one else could.

\* \* \*

Perhaps I was afraid to move on—I didn't want to let go of Tim. If grieving were the only way I could hold onto him, then I was determined to do it. But grieving *wasn't* the only way. He was in the boys. As Timmy grew older, his dad's mannerisms shined from within. The day of Timmy's first t-ball game, his chest swelled with pride as he scampered across the field wearing his crisp, white, mini-uniform— soon to be covered in grass-stains and dirt. Every part of me smiled.

## The Calm after the Storm

Almost two years had passed since we lost Tim. On the last day at my counselor's office, I walked out that door and breathed a deep sigh of relief. My eyes were opened beyond what the past held. I gazed at my surroundings. Life was beautiful and worth living again. The grass appeared greener. The sun's warmth seeped through me with promise. In that moment, I let go of Tim, knowing he would want me to move on. To live my life. I knew that I was ready—ready for whatever God had planned.

> **"You can't start the next chapter in your life
> if you keep re-reading the last one."**
> ~Author Unknown

As for meeting someone else to spend my life with, I really didn't have any big plans to do so.

135

"Lord, I'm not going to the bars, or going anywhere to look for anybody. If You want me to be a widow, I will be a widow the rest of my life," I prayed.

A smile surfaced as I continued, "But, if You do have someone for me, just put him on my doorstep."

Little did I know that this was exactly what God had in mind. Pete and his little girl were our neighbors when we met. We became friends, fell in love, and got married. We had another little girl together and have been married for thirty-one years. A wonderful man and extraordinary husband, he tells me every day that we had "yours" and "mine" … but now we have "ours." I really couldn't ask for more.

\* \* \*

I can honestly say that my heart has truly healed. I was even able to find the strength to forgive the man who took Tim from me. There wasn't any point in being bitter—bitter that he had killed my husband, or even bitter that he wasn't convicted. Only God knew the truth, and either way, it wouldn't bring Tim back to us. I had to let it go.

**"He heals the brokenhearted and binds their wounds."**
*Psalm 147:3*
*(NIV)*

I would never want to go through these events again. But, because they drew me closer to God, building an unimaginable, personal bond with Him, I will never regret it. I love the Lord with my whole heart, soul, and mind. I praise Him for each and every one of my blessings. He deserves all glory and honor, and someday, I'll get to thank Him in person. Life everlasting awaits those who believe—a place beyond our wildest dreams. Tim is there waiting for us. His smile said it all.

*Names or locations have been changed to protect those involved.

Reflection Questions

1. Kathy was honest regarding her anger toward God. Can you recall a time when you were angry with God? What was the result of that anger?

2. Have you ever sensed a "spiritual battle" taking place in your life? If so, what was your role in this battle? How did you handle that role?

3. Todd* asked a question many people have asked at one point or another: "If there is a God, how could He let such horrible things happen to good people?" Later, Kathy makes a powerful connection within her own moments of desperation, "God hadn't caused this—it was truly the devil." Why do we tend to question God's goodness or even His existence in the aftermath of pain? Could that contemplation also be a crucial part of the devil's plan?

4. "I know that you know what you know." Do you remember a clear moment when you knew something to be true, even if you couldn't explain why? How did that blind faith affect you as a person?

# The Watchman:
## Seeds of Growth

**Be relentless.**

Kathy had a difficult time understanding God's decision to take Tim, believing there could have been another way to ensure his salvation. Yet, she never rejected God. In fact, she held on to her faith, "knowing it was the only thing that would save me." She was angry and confused. But she was also relentless.

Most likely we can all relate to Kathy's anger, fear, desperation, and exhaustion. We may experience different causes and levels of intensity, but similar emotions. However, I find myself inspired by Kathy's tireless pursuit for her Cornerstone, her Father, despite her brokenness. No one knew Kathy better than her Creator. So why would she ever turn to anyone else? Kathy didn't know why God hadn't prevented her tears, and yet, she knew He was the only one she *wanted* to wipe them away. In return, God constantly reassured her that He was there. He was in the silence. In fact, often that's where we can hear Him most.

Why aren't we consistently pursuing God from our trenches? A ruthless circumstance may bring you to your worst, making you disoriented, desperate for a source to direct the smidgen of trust that remains. When everything appears to be failing us, it's easy to fool ourselves into believing our only certainty is the person staring back at us in the mirror.

It can be deceptively appealing to give up. To give up on our goals. To give up on those around us. To give up on God. After all, it takes less effort to concede than to endure. And why hold on to something or someone when we don't have one-hundred-percent certainty of life playing out exactly the way we desire? What's the point? The unfortunate truth is, if we decide to give up on God—on

His plan—then we didn't have absolute trust in Him in the first place. He is living up to His Word. If we abandon our faith, we're the ones not holding up our end of the bargain.

> **"When you feel like giving up, remember why**
> **you held on for so long in the first place."**
> ~Author Unknown

We are tested, over and over again, leaving us on a constant search for answers and solutions. It's true, we don't have one-hundred-percent certainty that life is going to play out the way we imagined. We will scrape bottom at some point on our journeys. But we *do* have certainty. *God* is our absolute certainty. Our sole source of unwavering support and comfort. Find your footing in His Word, our map when the road forks. Be relentless. Bury your head in His chest. In His wisdom. In the peace that He brings.

There's no safer place to be.

*"God is our refuge and strength, a very present help in trouble."*
*Psalm 46:1*
*(KJV)*

# CHAPTER 7

## The Well ~ Irresistible Love

*"If you want to walk on water, you've got to get out of the boat."*
~John Ortberg

*Author's Note: Narration in this testimony is shared by two men, Rob and Chris. As the story moves through time, the voice and perspective shifts from one person to the other, section by section.*

### Jolted (Rob)

O n August 22, 2002, I packed up my office. *This can't be happening. No. It's just a bad dream. I'm going to wake up. Any minute now ....*

\* \* \*

Fresh out of college, I began my career as a youth minister at a church with about 1,600 members. At first, it was seemingly a match made in heaven. We had an enormous youth group. The teens I worked with told me constantly how I was making a difference in their lives. Parents thanked me, saying I was taking the youth group deeper than it had ever gone before. All of this encouragement left me feeling like I was exactly where I needed to be. As a newly married couple, my wife and I were happy to be living out our calling in a wonderful place with wonderful people. We thought we'd never leave.

Every now and then when the regular preacher was absent, other ministers on the church staff were asked to give the sermon. So one Sunday night, I was given the opportunity to preach.

"You're a great youth minister, but you're an even better preacher! You have a real gift." I was told afterward by several people.

During the months that followed, I was given multiple opportunities to preach. After about the third time, one leader in the church even spoke to me about it.

"I could see you being the next preacher here one day," he confided.

I was teased with comments such as, "We hope you will stay here forever. You know we won't let you leave! We hope to bury you here!"

Well, they buried me all right ....

\* \* \*

Since I began in ministry, I've had a passion for reaching into the lives of people who didn't have any church context or, for whatever reason, had been alienated from the church. Being a compassionate and inclusive person by nature, I strove to find ways to include, accept, and embrace those in the community. I spoke boldly about those we should be reaching and took some intentional actions to connect with those on the margins. We had a group of outstanding teenagers in our youth group, mainly stemming from middle-to-upper-class families. I felt we needed to extend our reach in order to be more present and involved with those who might not feel comfortable coming into a church building or formal religious gathering.

> *"Leadership isn't falling in line – it's creating the line."*
> *~Author Unknown*

To advance this idea, I worked with a group of student leaders to host a three-on-three basketball and video game tournament, giving away prizes to the winners. My hope was to interact with inner-city guys who wouldn't show up at our building without a reason. Around thirty young men from the community came, followed by my youth-group planting a sign that night in each of the attendee's yards that read, "We're glad you were with us!" I beamed with joy. This was a strong step in the right direction.

"So you're bribing people to get them to come to church?" I was asked by a church leader the following week.

"Bribing? What do you mean? That's not at all what I was doing." I responded.

At work, I was continually challenged on my drive to reach others who were different or had made large mistakes in their pasts. But at home, I had an exciting distraction. That February, my wife Aimee and I were blessed with our first child, a baby girl. I was high on life, also having built and moved into a brand new house. But despite all the elation in my personal life, the tides in my career were turning. One evening, two weeks after Anna's birth, I was called into a meeting.

"You've got a pocket of people here who don't like the way you're doing things, Rob," an elder said.

My level of inclusiveness made some uncomfortable. If embracing those who didn't fit was the charge against me—I *was* guilty. I stood by my choices, making a powerful few *very* mad. It wasn't long before I was undermined.

> **"Silence in the face of evil is itself evil: God will not hold us guiltless. Not to speak is to speak. Not to act is to act."**
> *~Dietrich Bonhoeffer*

\* \* \*

It would be okay. Surely the elders would back me. They always had.

We met on occasion for three or four months to make sure the issue was dissolving. However, the group of influencers refused to let it go. They wanted me gone.

"Oh, don't worry about all of this! They love you. You'll be fine," Aimee said, trying to alleviate my concern.

"You don't understand how serious this is," I responded. "Some are determined to get rid of me."

But Aimee couldn't see it … until I made a declaration that finally grabbed her attention.

"I'm afraid you'll only understand the day a moving truck backs into our driveway. I have a feeling this is not going to end well."

"Are you kidding me? You think they're going to get rid of us? How could they? We've invested our *lives* here. This church is like a family to us!"

Aimee was just a new mom trying to figure things out. This was a curve ball neither she nor I was ready for. We both wanted to protect our family, but ended up being powerless.

In August, one of the elders called, requesting to meet for lunch at Red Lobster. "We're going to have to part ways, Rob."

I sat motionless, trying to make sense of his words as they lingered between us.

"You've done nothing wrong. But I'm afraid this just isn't going to work anymore."

\* \* \*

Many parents and teens were upset.

"We'll rise up! We'll rally and fight for your job," I was told.

"Though I appreciate your support more than you will ever know, please don't," I said.

Stirring people up, possibly causing a greater divide within the church, wouldn't benefit anyone.

Though I chose to leave peacefully, I was deeply wounded, nearly walking away from serving God within the confines of the church's institution. How could a church I had invested so much of my heart into simply be done with me? I wasn't just losing a job and my livelihood; I was losing my church family. After five and a half faithful years, I was out of a job. I now had a six-month-old, a newly built house for sale, and sure enough, a moving truck parked in our driveway. All I knew was to trust God, even when I couldn't understand. I took this as His way of moving me on. There had to be something else He was calling me to do.

**"Let us not become weary in doing good,**
**for at the proper time we will reap a harvest if we do not give up."**
*Galatians 6:9*
*(NIV)*

## Our Desert (Chris)

*My family and I uprooted from our friends and family in Oregon and moved to Idaho in February, 2005. I was taking on a new Lowe's Home Improvement store, where I would serve as the general manager. In our new Idaho location, we lived in an area primarily dominated by a faith other than our own. Those living in this area were great people—solid morals, strong fiber. However, it was a difficult community to break into. Many young families lived there, yet opportunities to foster new friendships were lacking. We were thankful for several families at church that made us feel welcome, becoming our Idaho family; but overall, Idaho could be a lonely place for us. I'd go to work, carrying on with life as usual. But outside of our church environment, solitude crept in.*

*Many nights my wife Nicki and I would discuss our situation. Our seclusion allowed us a lot of time to talk with each other, creating a bond that I loved. Not only that, but we spent a ton of time talking to God. As our prayer life increased, the more God spoke to us and opened doors when needed. When we started to ask the right questions, God provided the answers.*

**"You do not have because you do not ask God."**
*James 4:2*
*(NIV)*

In June of 2008, another opportunity arrived at a Lowe's store in Nashville, TN. We were excited to be near my family who lived only a few hours from Nashville. Our time in Idaho was lonely. Physically we were surrounded by people, and yet in our day-to-day walk, we were alone in a wilderness. But it was also our "desert time" with God—a crucial time in our walk of faith. My wife's and my growth was in Him and because of Him. We may have been isolated in our geographical location, but He never left us. In fact, He was our sole companion.

> **"Hardships often prepare ordinary people**
> **for an extraordinary destiny."**
> *~C.S. Lewis*

## A New Life in Nashville (Rob)

In 2008, I enrolled in a Missional Living graduate class at Lipscomb University in Nashville, TN. We explored the question: "What does the kingdom of God look like here and now, in our everyday midst?"

Professor Earl Lavender challenged us with a project: "I want you to write a paper on what the church would look like in an everyday environment, not just on Sunday morning in the church building."

I had been wrestling with this question for a long time. By this time I had worked in a church context for approximately twelve years, loving my work as a youth minister. Although deep down, I sensed the church was not being all it should be. It was as if we lived in a bit of a bubble, only reaching those who came from other churches or just happened to show up on Sunday mornings. I wanted to help the church. To figure out what it would look like to *be* church, aside from attending a service within four walls. To create a space where we could be relationally in the presence of people's lives—to love them.

Professor Lavender exposed us to the book, *The Shaping of Things to Come,* by Michael Frost and Alan Hirsch. This book reconsidered our institutional models, highlighting how Sunday mornings in our church buildings weren't going to work in the future. Europe had already experienced this, having empty churches on many corners. Some had even shifted worship gatherings into pubs, being very successful in doing so. We were in a post-modern age where people weren't looking for God within church structures (if they were looking for Him at all), whether we liked it or not.

Quickly, this paper developed into more than a class project. I started writing a vision, encompassing a modern-day coffee house. At a restaurant, people come and go. But at a coffee house, people willingly sit down and hang out. It was the perfect place to embody a community of people while allowing relationships to cultivate.

As I dove into the first few pages, I knew that this had to happen. My work was not just for a grade or an assignment. I sensed that God was calling me to actually do this. The more I wrote, the more I realized there was so much more I wanted to say. The project required twelve pages, but I couldn't stop there! I wrote twenty-seven.

As Professor Lavender handed me back my paper, he said, "This is really good, Rob. You could do this."

At first, I think Aimee thought I was crazy. Understandable, since outside of selling golf balls as a kid, I had absolutely zero business expertise. I had an undergraduate degree in Bible and a Master of Divinity in Theology. I managed a budget as youth minister, but had never started a business in my life! But despite that, Aimee always remained supportive.

"Well, if you ever do this, I'm behind you," she'd say, though probably never thinking it would happen.

But I believed Dr. Lavender was right—with God's help, I could do this. But when and how?

* * *

I sat on the coffee-house plan for about two years, waiting for God's timing. In 2010, my good friend, Brian Holaway, and I pulled out those dusty pages. We started exploring the concept of how we could incorporate a coffee house and our common passion to fight poverty.

Many of us ask ourselves, "How can we make a difference in this world?" We feel like we are here to do *something*. In search of the same answers, I indulged in the book, *The Hole in Our Gospel*, by Richard Stearns, which explored our lack of focus on what Jesus says about the world's wealth and poverty. Its pages captured me. The statistics were powerful, leaving me in awe of how blessed I was. Even though I'm not considered wealthy by America's standards, my family and I have more than that of ninety nine percent of the world's population[11].

"What if we gave the profits away, Rob? We'll just give it all away," Brian said.

"That's an amazing idea," I replied. "Let's measure our success, not by how much money we make, but how much we give away."

What if a company decided that the way of *being* the kingdom was through their business? Building a business model with the sole purpose of giving the profits away. It was a powerful concept. We agreed from that point forward: The coffee house would be non-profit, and its income would fight poverty around the world. Now of course, this alone couldn't end world poverty. Fighting poverty is a complicated endeavor. Corrupt systems can be involved. Corrupt governments. We may not be able to end world poverty, but we could do something about it.

We also knew a coffee house wouldn't make the kind of money that a corporation such as Microsoft or Apple would. But at the same time, statistics show the average American worker spending approximately 1,100 dollars a year on coffee.[12] We'll spend four dollars on a cup of coffee and yet, fifty five percent of the whole world lives on less than two dollars a day[13].

---

[11] Hugo, Gye. "America IS the 1%: You Need Just $34,000 Annual Income to be in the Global Elite ... and HALF the World's Richest People Live in the U.S." *Daily Mail*. Associated Newspapers Ltd., 5 January 2012. Web. 02 August 2015.

[12] Tuttle, Brad. "How Much You Spend Each Year on Coffee, Gas, Christmas, Pets, Beer, and More." *TIME*. TIME Inc., 23 January 2012. Web. 02 August 2015.

[13] Stearns, Richard. *The Hole in Our Gospel*. Nashville: Thomas Nelson, 2009. Print.

A clear path surfaced, integrating two things that pressed on my heart—the future of "the church," and fighting poverty. Not just to open a non-profit coffee house, but to create a church community within it. The business *itself* was the mission—the vehicle advancing the kingdom of God. This wasn't just a random idea. *God* provided this revelation, and now was the time to bring it to reality. Brian and I had heard of a coffee house called Ebenezer's in Washington D.C. that was very similar to what we wanted to do. It was established by author Mark Batterson.

The next thing I knew, Brian was on his way to Washington.

The staff at Ebenezer's was very helpful.

"If you want to do this, we'll help you with some inside information to get you started," Brian was told.

Upon his return, we met to discuss the details and reassess where we stood. However, every time we began to advance in our steps, doors wouldn't open. We hit constant brick walls with financing and location. Things just weren't falling into place. So the project plan returned to my desk drawer. But hope wasn't lost. I'd never been so sure of something—that if I just trusted, when the time was right, He would show me how to get there.

\* \* \*

Toward the end of 2011, I caught word that Chris, a friend of mine from church, had lost his job. Somehow everything came back to me in a single moment. Coffee-house idea … Chris! I grabbed my phone and quickly began texting Brian: "You're not going to believe this, but I think our coffee-house vision just took on new life. There's a guy at our church—you may know him. He worked for Lowe's and has a lot of management experience. I think he could be interested. What do you think?"

"Great! Let's put it back on the table," Brian shot back.

No time to waste.

## Intrigue (Chris)

*By now, I had worked for Lowe's Home Improvement for twelve years, the last three years as general manager in Nashville. During the past several years I received multiple management and community-development awards from the company. All of my hard work was paying off. However, despite that, due to a transition and repositioning of management, Lowe's let me go. Though I was exhausted from years of fifty-to-ninety hour weeks, losing my job was devastating. But I couldn't let those feelings slow me down. I dove into the job search, interviewing for other big-box retailers.*

*Then one day at church, Rob, our youth minister, approached me.*

*"Man, I'm so sorry for what you've been through. I've lost a job too, so I can understand how you're feeling. And I'm not sure if this is too soon, Chris, but since you're kind of in the "in-between" right now, what do you think about doing something a little bit different?"*

*Rob elaborated on an idea for a business, a coffee shop whose profits would support missions.*

*"What would you think about the next step in your life just being ... sort of exploring. You have the expertise from a management standpoint. What if you're the guy to help make this happen?"*

*I'd never heard of anything like this before. After doing nothing but retail for eighteen years, I almost wanted to be out of that line of work for a while. Retail is a whole different ballgame, at times seeing the mean side of others. Customers tended to treat employees as if they were of a lower class than they were, often demanding assistance rather than asking. But I was honestly skeptical of the plan. The coffee-house concept was so different. I couldn't quite piece it all together. I needed to think this through and pray about it.*

*My focus remained on finding another full-time job, more worried about providing for my family than hearing about the prospects of doing something outside of the box. But despite that, during the following weeks my thoughts continually veered toward Rob's idea. I wasn't sure it would pan out, but we'd never know unless we tried. And if I were going to continue in retail, this was definitely a positive way to give back to The Kingdom. So I gave Rob a call.*

> **"What we are is God's gift to us.**
> **What we become is our gift to God."**
> **~Anonymous**

Rob, Brian, and I met at church to discuss the full plan. I walked away that day still very cautious. It was a massive notion to chew on. During the next two weeks, in between job interviews, I researched. Read about the coffee industry. Uncovered statistics. Played with numbers. Brainstormed the possibilities. I couldn't help myself! And after all of my digging, the details started to add up. This might actually work!

Over Thanksgiving dinner, I shared the coffee-house idea with my extended family.

"Man, that is exciting! I want to know more about it," my brother-in-law said.

The rest of my family's reaction was a little different.

"You're thinking of doing what? ...What? I don't understand ...."

I was torn. I prayed, asking God if this was the right thing to do. Was it right for my family? Nicki thought I was crazy even looking into it. She wasn't working at that time and was busy homeschooling our children. Her concerns revolved around providing for our family and keeping our house. I couldn't blame her for that, and I was right there with her. You give up security when trying to start a business. There's no guarantee it's going to work. Rob, Brian, and I weren't in this to make money, but we still had to take care of our families. This could be just a mediocre investment with a mediocre opening, and a couple of months later we'd be out of business. It was a gamble. But was this what God wanted? Could I persuade Nicki to think I wasn't going insane?

> **"If you aren't in over your head, how do you know how tall you are?"**
> ~*T.S. Eliot*

*The more I met with Rob and Brian, the more I loved the idea. I didn't know if we would be successful, but what I did know is that I wanted to pursue it. I was willing to take the risk.*

## Refinement (Rob)

Brian, Chris, and I worked very hard at refining the vision. We had a smooth synergy between us, and once again, I awoke every morning with momentum streaming through my veins. Our footing was strong. With God as our strength, we could do this.

Two or three weeks in January passed when Chris and I received an e-mail:

"I can't explain it. I just feel like God has released me from this desire. But I wish you guys the best on this journey. I know this is going to be successful. Please press on," Brian wrote.

At that particular phase in his life, Brian believed that God was calling him elsewhere. He was respectfully and graciously stepping out of the equation. I tried to talk him out of it. "Are you *sure* you're hearing from God correctly on this? Won't you reconsider?"

Brian was not only a great friend but also an original co-founder. I didn't want to see him go.

"No, I can't explain it other than it's just God telling me it's not for me anymore."

Who could argue with that? Yet, I couldn't help but think, *oh man, God, what are you doing!* But Chris and I clung to the vision passionately. We moved forward, building a team with four other guys who became our board, each sacrificing time with their families to get this dream off the ground. God knew a diverse group with many different skill-sets was necessary, and He succeeded in providing it.

* * *

The coffee house's name needed to embody everything we wanted to portray. In the book of John, Chapter 4, Jesus meets a Samaritan woman at the well. This woman had five previous husbands and was not married to the man with whom she currently lived. Being a Samaritan, she was looked down upon, hated and despised, considered to be a half-breed by the other Jews. On top of that, women had very little rights or a voice in society, giving her even less clout. After speaking with Jesus, she left that well not fully understanding who she had met, just knowing she had made a powerful encounter. Returning to her village, she proclaimed she had met the Messiah! Jesus didn't give her all the answers, but he left her with the most important thing—*a piece of hope.*

> **"Jesus answered, 'Everyone who drinks this water will be thirsty again, but whoever drinks the water I give them will never thirst. Indeed, the water I give them will become in them a spring of water welling up to eternal life.'"**
> *John 4:13-14*
> *(NIV)*

The Samaritan woman represented exactly whom we wanted to reach within the coffee house—anyone with a difficult past, from all walks of life. We wanted to provide hope that Jesus is who He says He is. Not to preach, but to engage and build relationships so that customers would leave asking the same type of questions the Samaritan woman asked: "Could Jesus really be the Messiah? Is that what Jesus looks like today—a place that is loving and respectful, caring about the poor and oppressed?"

That was a tall order. We wouldn't claim to do it perfectly, but just to do the best we could at being living, breathing, hands and feet of Jesus—not under a religious denomination, but under His leadership alone.

> **"May the bread on your tongue leave a trail of crumbs,**
> **to lead the hungry back to the place that you are from."**
> *~Derek Webb, Take to the World*

Poverty was also still a focus. A lot of areas needed to be addressed concerning poverty—food crisis, disease, etc. It was important to be practical, deciding where to focus our efforts. We realized that one of the greatest needs was simply water. The statistics haunted us: 6,000 children die every single day from a lack of clean water[14]. It's not that people were dying of thirst. They were dying of water-borne illnesses from drinking contaminated water. An epidemic existed over something that could be resolved. Therein lay our answer. We would build clean-water systems.

> **"The water and sanitation crisis claims more lives**
> **through disease than any war claims through guns."**
> *~Reported by Water.org*

We partnered with a local well-drilling team called The Living Water Project[15]. They provided the direct drilling or contracted out the drilling of wells. Wells could be built around the world for as little as 1,000 dollars and as expensive as approximately 18,000 dollars (depending on the location, its economy, and well depth). Every single cent collected was directed toward building and maintaining wells. Once the building of a well is complete, a committee is put into place within the benefitted community to guard, protect, and manage the well. If it needs repair, the committee contacts The Living Water Project team. These details provided confidence that our donations would support our goal to the fullest.

---

[14] "How Poor Sanitation Kills the Equivalent of 20 Planes Full of Children Every Day." *The Guardian*. Guardian News and Media Limited or its affiliated companies, 31 May 2003. Web. 02 August 2015.

[15] The Living Water Project: http://www.livingwaterwells.com/

Our board devoted ourselves to this vision, while finalizing the name for our coffee house: The Well. It encompassed everything we wanted to be and do. We would strive to be a meeting place representing Jesus, in addition to being a well, a clean-water source of life for the world, building as many as we could—everywhere. We completely surrendered that plan to God.

"We need all the know-how, all the provisions You can give us, Lord."

## A Skewed Perspective (Chris)

*Mixed reactions continued to roll in. We heard anything from, "This is really cool," to, "Why would you do that?" People weren't necessarily opposed to the idea, but a lot of them were skeptical. Our whole idea pointed toward making a decision to be different. The reactions from others assured us that we were accomplishing that goal, if nothing else.*

> **"Remember, you can't make a difference unless you are different."**
> *~Birdsong & Heim; @stickyJesus*

*We saw The Well's potential. We saw how it could change the world. But we had to be practical. When starting a business, you don't make a lot of money initially. The majority of the profits go back into the business. We prayed, hoped, and crossed our fingers that we would have only a small season of drought. But either way, we needed to be ready for it. In preparation, family sacrifices had to be made.*

*It was difficult, but also eye-opening, learning our wants versus our needs. Coming from almost a six-figure income and plummeting to almost nothing came with large life adjustments. Our priorities had to shift. Dave Ramsey's envelope system came in handy (allocating cash into categorized envelopes in order to maintain a monthly budget), not to mention clipping coupons. Beans and rice were often on the menu. We cut off cable and stopped eating out. Movie-theater trips turned into Redbox® nights.*

*"What are you doing that for?" we'd hear from friends.*

*"Well, it's a sacrifice. This is what we want to do."*

*That's really all there was to it. We had to learn to do things differently, trying to be more conscientious of how we spent our dollars. We may have appeared crazy, but sometimes "crazy" can be rewarding.*

**"Here's to the crazy ones."**
~Apple Inc.

*However, sacrifices came in the form of more than just materials. I didn't have much time to spend with my family when I was at Lowe's, and I'm not saying I had a lot more while working on the coffee house. The hours devoted to get The Well up and running appeared endless at times. Add that to home-schooling our kids and Nicki going back to work full time. It was a recipe for chaos. Between the two of us, we basically had three full-time jobs.*

*But despite our constant quest for balance, I couldn't overlook the benefits. I was learning who my kids were—details I would never know if they were in public school and I was working in a major-retail box. Our connection grew very strong. They were exposed to The Well's mission, not to mention absorbing the literal effects of our new, limited lifestyle. At night we'd stop to pray. I'd hear them praying for people who were sick in other parts of the world. For people who didn't have clean water. For people who didn't have the necessities of life. I was in awe.*

*In America, we have a skewed perspective. It's easy to become immersed into our lifestyles, often assuming everybody in the world lives as we do. Even if The Well didn't take off, it was changing my family's lives—our viewpoints. To hear our seven-year-old pray for someone who didn't have water reinforced our footing. We didn't have to wait for our sacrifices to pay off—they already had.*

**"Lack of access to clean water and sanitation kills children at a rate equivalent of a jumbo jet crashing every four hours."**
~Reported by Water.org

* * *

*So the project continued. We needed to investigate different locations for The Well. Neither Rob nor I had ever worked in the real-estate market. Did we want to be south of town, west of town, east of town? Our days consisted of driving from property to property. Out of nearly forty buildings we viewed, ten or twelve looked promising. But after talking to realtors, discovering the outrageous monthly payments, plus a five-year lease commitment, we were back on the road. We didn't even know if this was going to work ... how could we possibly sign a five-year agreement?*

*The search continued. "God, please make something clear."*

## Burger King, Anyone? (Rob)

**"Inspiration exists, but it must find you working."**
*~Pablo Picasso*

We needed to be different. We couldn't just "talk" about wanting to change the world—we had to actually *do* it. But first, we needed money. The board members and I stared at the dollar figure in disbelief. Approximately 100,000 dollars was necessary to get The Well off the ground. *None* of us had that kind of money—not even close! Between the six of us, we scraped up as much as we could through *tremendous* sacrifice, totaling approximately 25,000 dollars. It wasn't enough.

This is impossible. We need a location. We need a building. We need supplies. We need staff. That list certainly won't be accomplished with only 25,000 dollars!

The target amount was far beyond our reach, but that didn't stop our feet from moving. While hunting for The Well's location, the board heard through the grapevine of a potential place in affluent Green Hills. An old, vacant Burger King was being leased around the corner from the owner's flower mart ... and the owner just happened to be Bob.

About seven years prior, I took our youth group on a mission trip to Jamaica. One of the adults who accompanied the group brought his friend Bob along. Bob and I got along great. We were alike in character, had the same birthday, and to top it off, both possessed shiny, shaved heads. Despite our best intentions, Bob and I had very little interaction after arriving home from the trip. Life took over.

But it didn't matter who had ownership—no way could we afford that place! It was way out of our league. Regardless of that assumption, it was worth the investigation. So I arranged a meeting with good ol' Bob.

On a frigid February morning, I made the left-hand turn into the Burger King parking lot. I prayed constantly before the meeting, "God, please, if there's any chance we can get a space to lease that would be favorable, let this be it."

It was the *perfect* location. But I wasn't hiding from reality. A building this size in this part of town would require a 10-12K per month lease. As much as this would benefit us, it probably wasn't possible. And on top of that, would Bob even remember me? Would I recognize him after all these years?

I stepped into the crisp air and marched toward the building. A man in the parking lot shouted toward me, "Hey! There's my birthday brother! How you doing, Rob? That trip we took together was great, wasn't it?"

The pace of my heart slowed. It was as if seven years hadn't passed.

"Come on in! Let me show you the space," Bob said.

Bob, Chris, and I shuffled through the building. It looked pretty dilapidated, filled with Bob's flowers and storage materials, while still resembling the old Burger King décor. But despite that, I saw what it could become.

> **"Every block of stone has a statue inside it and it is the task of the sculptor to discover it. The sculptor's hand can only break the spell to free the figures slumbering in the stone."**
> *~Michelangelo*

"Well, Bob, let us tell you about our plans for this place. This is not about us. We want to make money and then give it away."

I continued with the details, praying that our goals would resonate with his. Bob listened thoughtfully. As we approached the end of our conversation, he said, "That's great, guys. Wonderful."

He didn't tip his hand. And yet, the glimmer in his eye revealed his wheels turning.

He continued, "Well, I'll tell you what ... maybe we can work something out for you to lease this place."

We waited for the number. What was it going to be? Seven thousand a month? Eight thousand?

"How about ... mmmm ... 2,000 dollars a month. Could you do that?" Bob asked.

Chris and I shot glances toward each other. Did he say what I thought he just said? We'd *find* a way! But no matter how much I wanted to, we still didn't have enough money for me to confidently respond with, "Tell us where to sign!"

We did our best to play it cool.

"That sounds amazing, Bob. We would love to do that. But let us go back and pray about it and see what we can come up with," I replied.

God had given us a gift, a sign to forge ahead. But it was time for us to step it up.

\* \* \*

After studying a lot of Jewish culture, I found myself reflecting upon the story of a rabbi named Choni[16]. Around 30 or 40 B.C, just before Jesus' birth, a severe drought threatened to wipe out Israel. Choni knew what needed to be done. He knelt down on the ground, drawing a circle around himself. Standing in the middle with his staff in hand, he prayed aloud a very bold prayer: "God, I will not leave this circle until you send rain for our people."

---

[16] Young, Brad H. *Jesus the Jewish Theologian.* Peabody: Hendrickson Publishers, 1995. Print.

The Pharisees ridiculed him, saying, "How dare you talk to God that way!"

But Choni remained in his circle, praying relentlessly, day after day. According to the legend, the rain started to fall very gently. This was good news. But after ten months of drought, it wasn't enough.

Choni once again stood in the middle of that circle and shouted, "God, not for this kind of rain have I prayed, but for a life-giving rain! Please send the rain!"

The drops from above increased, becoming a torrential downpour. What looked like the beginning of a flood caused people to dart for safety, fearing for their lives. But Choni wasn't going anywhere. He stood firm in the downpour, shouting, "Lord, not for *this* type of rain, but for a *life-giving* rain so that we can replenish our crops and save our lives!"

The rain slowed, turning into a steady, generous shower. God's people were saved! The Pharisees were still angry about Choni's bold prayer, but to others, Choni was a hero, and an example of how God invites us to pray.

> **"Heroes are made by the paths they choose,**
> **not the powers they are graced with."**
> ~Brodi Ashton

This story had always resonated with me, inspiring me to teach it to my students at Lipscomb University. However, the day the words from *The Circle Maker* by Mark Batterson leapt toward me from a book shelf, my game of connect the dots began.

"What in the world?" I said.

I reached for the paperback, shocked that someone may have elaborated on a short story that few had ever read. It couldn't be. And yet it was. Batterson, the very man who opened Ebenezer's in Washington D.C., had turned Choni's story into a full-fledged book on praying boldly around our Godly visions, encircling our dreams in prayer.

The churches in which I was raised weren't very charismatic. I had grown used to prayer being a very solemn experience. So this type of prayer was extremely out of the ordinary for me. Though I was always open to talking to God in different ways, I wasn't raised to pray this way. But Choni's prayer didn't seem too different from some of Jesus' bold words about prayer. I was ready to "ask, seek, and knock." I bought *The Circle Maker* for all of our board members.

"Guys, here's what I want us to do. I want us to pray circles. It's going to be uncomfortable at first, but God has given us this vision and it's time for us to pray for Him to give us the provision. We now know we have a potential space. I think he wants us to pray boldly for this place. Let's pray circles."

## Dry-Erase Prayers (Chris)

*I'd been raised in a church my whole life. Prayer had been important, but it's never been something that was directive—speaking to exactly what you wanted. The Circle Maker directed praying in a way that had never crossed my mind. We were moved by the book's strategy, drawing circles around what we desired. I knew God heard and answered prayer, although His response may not always be yes.*

*The door had just opened to a great piece of property in Green Hills. Ever since I moved to Nashville I had avoided Green Hills. It was always so busy! But now, ironically, did God want me there full time? Was this location really what God was telling us to secure? We were motivated to pray for exactly that. And if this was the place, we prayed for the money to make it happen. I was very curious to see God's response to this approach, knowing we were truly seeking His way and not our own.*

*So on Wednesday, March 1st, 2012, around 8:30 p.m., I headed to the old Burger King. I pulled out my black dry-erase marker and wandered around the pitch-black parking lot. The words from* The Circle Maker *emerged from my mind. I needed to call out and say specifically what I wanted. I covered the windows with key scriptures from Isaiah and Jeremiah, speaking of making a claim for God, Him hearing our prayers, and answering accordingly. I called on His name, asking Him to do for the people. That's all we wanted to do in the first place—to create a space to help others.*

**"I promise you what I promised Moses:**
**'Wherever you set foot, you will be on land I have given you—"**
Joshua 1:3
(NLT)

*For almost two hours I circled the building, praying and listening to see if God's response was, "Do it." Just as I was getting ready to leave, Rob pulled into the parking lot, ready to do the very same thing.*

**"The value of consistent prayer is not that He**
**will hear us, but that we will hear Him."**
~William McGill

## Now Go Do It (Rob)

At around 10:30 p.m., I marched over to the side of the building next to the entrance, knelt down on the asphalt, and began my circle. Earlier, I had rummaged through my wife's teaching closet for a piece of chalk. The best I could find was a white piece, only about two inches in length. I hoped it would be enough. After a few yards, I realized this was going to be a harder task than I had assumed.

Slowly and deliberately I crawled, etching the circle around the 2,400 square foot building. Sadly, I had vastly underestimated how much chalk was needed, running out after only circling half of the structure. Reminded of my inadequacies, I slumped down on the ground as I shouted in frustration, "I can't even finish my circle!"

I tried to remind myself that God gets the point. I knew there was nothing magical about this circle, yet I wanted so badly to finish it. I *needed* to finish it. My gaze fell to the asphalt as I spotted a white rock lying only a couple feet away. *Hmmm … would it work?* I reached for the rock with determination, pressing it firmly against the ground. It was a lot harder to use than chalk, but it worked! I continued to carve my circle, finishing the loop inch by inch.

Once the rock finally collided with my initial chalk line, I prepared to pray like I had never prayed before. I placed my hands on the windows and projected my words to the heavens.

"God, I want lives to be changed inside here. Just like you tore down the walls of Jericho, would you please give us this place? Would you send life-giving rain, allowing us to turn this building into a place of living water that fills the wells and quenches the thirsty souls right here in our city?"

> **"When the trumpets sounded, the army shouted,**
> **and at the sound of the trumpet, when the men**
> **gave a loud shout, the wall collapsed; so everyone**
> **charged straight in, and they took the city."**
> *Joshua 6:20*
> *(NIV)*

I prayed more boldly and faithfully then I ever had. And Chris and I weren't the only ones. Each board member prayed individually around the building as well. We were just *that* convicted.

\* \* \*

Through March and into April, we prayed, planned, and prayed some more. But we still didn't have the money. Something inside of me stirred, surfacing the name of a specific church member. Maybe he'd want to invest? Great guy. Strong Christian. His kids were in my youth group and I knew him well enough to know that he might see the value in what we were pursuing. But despite that, because I'm not a "business" guy, a 25,000 dollar request was outrageously overwhelming to me. Not to mention I *hate* asking for money. But I couldn't walk away from this opportunity. It was as if God were saying, "You prayed and I want to provide. But I'm not going to drop it out of the sky. Now go ask the very person I've put on your heart!"

I had no idea what the response would be, but thankfully, he was open to meeting at the Burger King.

We strolled throughout the building. As I finished describing our plan, I said, "Kevin, that's what we think God is leading us to do here. And, um … we need about 25,000 dollars to do it." I couldn't believe the words actually came out of my mouth.

His eyes widened as he met my gaze and then peered around the room once more. "Wow. Okay, well, I'll have to take a look at some things and give this a lot of thought, Rob."

"I completely understand. Please take as much time as you need."

As Kevin walked out that door, a hollow ache settled in the pit of my stomach. *Aw, I made a fool of myself. I just asked this guy who has kids in my youth group. He knows I'm a youth minister, not a business man. He'll never do it.*

Two weeks passed. Still no word. At the beginning of the third week, my office phone rang.

"Rob, this is Kevin. I've been thinking a lot about what you said. I just really love the plan. I want to give you 10,000 dollars outright. I also have a piece of property that I want to sell. I think I can make about 5,000 dollars on that. So, I'll give you what I make on that property to get you up to fifteen."

I could hardly believe what I was hearing!

"Then, I would like to give you a 10,000 dollar no-interest loan to put you at 25,000 dollars," Kevin concluded.

Time froze as I struggled to convince myself I was awake. No more questioning. No more doubt. I hung up the phone and dropped to my knees. With tears in my eyes, I cried out, "Thank you, God! Thank you. This has only happened because of *You*."

I felt as if I were standing in the rain, arms and hands wide open. I could literally *feel* God—His warm smile shining down on us, providing affirmation, and nudging us onward.

That day, March 22, just happened to be World Water Day—a day the United Nations had set aside to raise awareness about the need for clean water for millions of people around the world. For The Well, we would remember it as the day God provided the rain, making a five-year ambition a reality.

> **"Some people feel the rain. Others just get wet."**
> ~Bob Marley

\* \* \*

People continued to donate—ten dollars here, fifteen dollars there. An occasional 1,000 dollars. We even received one hundred sacrificial dollars from one of my freshman students. Added to the money our board members threw in, that brought us just over 50,000 dollars. Normally you wouldn't start a business with that kind of money. But God had been continually saying, "Trust Me. I will give you what you need if you just trust Me." So that's what we did. On March 23, 2012, we signed the lease on the good old Burger King.

Chris' managerial know-how and my theological vision came together naturally, providing a great starting point. We needed a good product. A mediocre cup of coffee would only hold up for so long, and our customers shouldn't have to settle. We even wanted the design to speak to what The Well would be—the bigger story. We wanted a comfortable place with reclaimed materials, because that's exactly what we are as people—we are repurposed—scrap wood that God picked up and turned into something special. Chris worked tirelessly to make that happen, throwing himself into The Well's construction.

## Coffee, Sweat, and Inspections (Chris)

*The day we signed the lease, Rob and I were on cloud nine. It was a twenty-four month lease with the option of extending an additional twelve months. We met Bob at the building, took care of the paperwork, and got the keys to what would become The Well. Our dream was becoming reality!*

*The camera clicked. Rob and I stood on the front patio with the keys to The Well in hand. But the minute that photo was taken, things changed. I was incredibly joyous. Yet at the same time, scared to death. Now we were responsible for making our lease payment and everything that came with it. It was a lot like buying your first car or house. When you finally sign that paper, you're thrilled—but on the flip-side you're thinking, I've gotta pay this thing off! There was a lot of work to be done.*

> **"Start by doing what's necessary, then what's possible, and suddenly you are doing the impossible."**
> *~St. Francis of Assisi*

\* \* \*

*First, we needed to work on the aesthetics of the interior. The dull wood and gold color that covered the Burger King's walls were terrible. Both had to go. We wanted The Well to be warm and inviting, while having a laid-back feel. So Walt Malone, a board member, brought in a friend, Laura Copeland, to help with the design.*

*"Maybe we could put something over top of the original wood?" Walt asked.*

*"What if we put barn wood over top, giving it a country-chic-type look?" Laura added.*

*Before we knew it, Matt Yates, another board member and Craigslist fanatic, located a barn for 700 dollars.*

*"Let's do it!" the team agreed.*

*We purchased the barn and headed out to the rural area with five volunteers. The tin on top was pulled off piece by piece, followed by the boards that supported each side. Approximately four days later, we headed back to Green Hills with our new décor in tow.*

*Board members, family, friends, and countless others piled into*

*The Well's parking lot. For the next week and a half, each piece of wood was refurbished. We cleaned every board, removed nails, and then applied a treatment to ensure all were bug-free. Our days were long, consuming every daylight hour with only fleeting nights to recharge. However, we had only just begun.*

*The next six months demanded even more from us while designing and reconstructing the materials into tables, shelves, counters, and signs. One-hundred-percent volunteer labor made this possible. We appreciated every hammered nail, every sturdy arm, and every swept floor. Even my kids pitched in once summer break started. It was a sacrifice for all of us, but more importantly, completely worthwhile.*

\* \* \*

We wanted people to come to The Well and believe in the mission of what we were trying to accomplish. But in order to get them through the door, a quality product had to be provided. We needed others to see a viable foundation. In order to do that, major research was on our horizon.

I had been a coffee fanatic for a while, but never to the point where I knew enough to teach or train. While gaining knowledge from a roaster in Pennsylvania, we read every book we could get our hands on. Then in April, an owner of Just Love Coffee Roasters in Murfreesboro, TN, dropped by The Well to offer a tasting. Their coffee was great, packed with the flavor that we desired for our customers.

Just Love took us under their wing. Having a local facility was an advantage, but they were not only our distributor. We shadowed, trained, and worked alongside their team, eventually sending our baristas to do the same.

Then came the equipment. Researching what The Well needed was daunting. We didn't know exactly what we should or should not use. Just when we thought Just Love couldn't be any more gracious, they extended their hand even further.

"Hey, you guys already have your equipment? If not, would you like our help?" a team member offered.

*Not only was every piece of equipment carefully selected with Just Love's help, but they also sent their techs to assist with proper installment. More prayers answered.*

\* \* \*

*And then the feared inspections began. Bob had initially warned us about the building. Apparently its inability to pass codes was a large reason it had remained deserted, providing concern from the start. To open our 2,400 square foot building, we had to submit a drawing of the location and everything housed inside. Upon submitting our layout to the fire marshal, we were automatically denied occupancy.*

*"You're over fire-code limit. For a retail or sit-down environment, there must be seven square feet for every person in the building. If your square footage exceeds one hundred people, you must have a fire-suppression system."*

*This was an enormous road-block, guaranteed to shut us down. A fire-suppression system was a 50,000 dollar expense. We most definitely did not have the means to do it. Not to mention, the building would eventually be torn down, so nobody was going to put that kind of money into it. I decided to visit the codes department to see if there were any options we were overlooking.*

*One of the guys in the office called me over. "Hey, let me help you. I know you guys are a non-profit. You just need to specify a lot of details exactly the right way. For example, are you going to have any retail space in the coffee house?"*

*"Well, sort of. We have some shelves where we were going to display our coffee products," I replied.*

*"That's a great start. You'll just need to add a bit more. The inclusion of retail space increases the square footage allotment from seven to fifteen square feet per person. We just have to work within the code specifications. That should take care of your fire-suppression system issue," he explained with a grin.*

* * *

*"We need to come up with some retail ideas for the store in order to obey codes," I said to the board.*

*Selling additional products on our shelves had never crossed our minds. And what products? Two days after we were told we needed to add more retail, we were contacted by an intern who had recently returned from India, working with a group called JOYN[17]. She had thought our missions sounded similar, prompting her to reach out. The answer to our retail problem, selling hand-made products by men and women in underdeveloped countries, was literally placed in our inbox.*

*"Wow, we could really bring awareness to other non-profits by providing a place to sell their products," I said.*

*The timing couldn't have been a coincidence. But how did she even find out about us? We had never met her before, nor have we met her since. We responded to her e-mails, offering free cups of coffee upon the opening of The Well, hoping we could meet and hear about her experiences in India. No response. Thankfully, our relationship continued to grow with JOYN, though the mystery remained as to the person who connected us.*

* * *

*Code inspections were extremely strict. At every turn, we hit a brick wall, each time with a different inspector. But they loved the mission. We never received a flat out, "No, this is not going to happen." The inspectors didn't look the other way, but each showed us how to quickly fix the issues without investing a lot of money. Again, our needs were met.*

## Joyning Forces (Rob)

God continued to bring us vendors. After *JOYN* came *Mission Lazarus[18]*.

---

[17] JOYN: http://www.joynindia.com/
[18] Mission Lazarus: http://www.missionlazarus.org/#welcome-home

"We would like to know if we can sell our merchandise in your coffee shop?"

"Um, we kind of *need* to sell your items," I said, shocked at the timing.

We were gearing up to sell bags, scarves, bracelets, journals, and many other hand-crafted products made by people on the streets of Honduras, Ethiopia, Uganda, and India. Some of these men and women lived on less than one dollar a day. The money made from these purchases prevented their return to the streets, pulling them out of poverty almost instantly. As long as the non-profit approaching us supported the cause to fight poverty (local or abroad), we were happy to support them. Coffee was now only part of our story.

And there came that question again: "How do I make a difference?" God was highlighting a way. Whether it be wearing our scarves, or sipping our coffee, that difference was going to be made. We were ready to ask people to consciously choose where to spend their money. Our customers would have the option of frequenting the coffee shop down the road, helping turn millionaires into billionaires, or come to The Well and help save lives. It was just that simple.

### Whispers (Chris)

*God was all around us, always two steps ahead. He was speaking to us, though sometimes we were in a rush to force situations to fit our perceptions and ideas. We would hit wall after wall, looking for alternatives to get out of our jams, struggling for a way to get through. To make things work. Every time we tried to force things to happen, we were stopped in our tracks. But when we slowed down to listen, something would nudge us from inside whispering, "What about this?" We realized the suggested route wasn't where we had been headed, and at the same time, it was where we needed to go.*

**"Whether you turn to the right or to the left, your ears will hear a voice behind you, saying, 'This is the way; walk in it.'"**
*Isaiah 30:21*
*(NIV)*

*Our human reaction is to trust God as long we know what's going to happen next. This journey was teaching us the opposite—we had to trust, even when we had no idea what was in store. Our Grand Opening was coming and I knew that the outcome might not be what we had hoped. But His plan was the one that mattered.*

## Grand Opening? (Rob)

A month before opening, Charlie, another one of our board members, and I were brainstorming at The Well.

"I want to create a place where people can share needs," I said.

I had been inspired by the early church to create a community that takes care of each other (Acts 2 and 4). If someone couldn't pay a tax or supply food to his family, the community shared. Because of this, there was seldom any need.

Overhearing our discussion, Chris said, "What if we turn this wall into a Needs Board where people can share their needs?"

In that moment, The Wishing Well wall was born.

\* \* \*

The next few weeks flew by. Before we knew it, it was Tuesday, July 10, 2012, the eve of opening night. With it being one of the hottest summers on record and college students out of town on summer break, we expected to use July and August to slowly ramp up into a "busy" September. Yet still, the day before opening was jam-packed with last-minute preparations. Excitement and apprehension played on our hearts as Laura, one of our team members, wrote menu items on the chalkboard.

*Were we really ready?* We had posted on Facebook that we would open the following morning at six o'clock, so at that point, there was no turning back. The very last thing on my to-do list was to create and print The Wishing Well cards, requesting a description of the person's need and contact information. I arrived home around 1:00 a.m., finished up the cards, and then climbed into bed, knowing I'd have to head back to The Well in about three hours.

Despite not being a morning person, my alarm clock quickly yanked me from slumber. The image of officially opening The Well's doors propelled my body out of our house by five o'clock. Nothing could slow me down. I arrived at 5:45 sharp and placed the cards on the shelf below The Wishing Well wall. And that was it. Everything was in place. The day I had been dreaming about for so long was here. Now for the big question: Would anybody come?

I stood in front of the order counter waiting eagerly for the first customer. The clock struck 5:59 a.m. when the door opened. The very first supportive face to enter belonged to a student from my first youth group where I had lost my job ten years before. Having moved to Nashville, she discovered us on Facebook and decided to pay a visit. We posed for a picture: The Well's very first customer. How unbelievably fitting.

The floodgates opened. I stood in that exact same spot from 5:59 a.m. until 5:00 or 6:00 p.m. I barely moved, attempting to greet and thank every single customer who walked through our door. They just kept coming, a mixture of those we knew and total strangers.

Around 3:00 that afternoon, Earl Lavender, my professor (and now colleague) whose project inspired The Well's vision, walked in. He slowly gazed around the room, taking in all that we had done, finally shuffling toward me. "This is good work, Rob."

I stood tall, grinning from ear to ear as Earl and I posed for a picture—one of my most prized possessions.

For about twelve hours straight I stood there, eagerly extending my hand. I met hundreds of people, engaging in countless conversations. I didn't eat lunch. I didn't eat anything. Not one encounter would be taken for granted. I've rarely been as proud in all of my life—proud to participate in something that I knew God had so clearly orchestrated.

## Block-Party Survival (Chris)

*Opening day was busy, but nothing compared to what was coming that Friday with Blood:Water Mission[19]. Blood:Water is a non-profit entity, supporting AIDS prevention and education in Africa, as well as installing clean-water systems throughout the world. Every summer, the mission raises money and awareness by organizing a bike tour, spanning from the west coast to the east coast of the United States. We were looking forward to doing work with Blood:Water in the future, so upon hearing they needed a place to stop, relax, and rejuvenate during the tour, we eagerly provided The Well as their location.*

*Friday morning started out like any other morning. Around noon, the Blood:Water internal team arrived and began preparing the parking lot for the bicyclists. Three or four additional groups joined shortly after to set up tables. Three food trucks parked and began prepping. We only had a trickling of customers during the next few hours, allowing us the extra time to prepare for what we didn't realize was coming.*

*Around three o'clock, vendors were talking amongst themselves, far from busy. By four o'clock, about fifty to sixty people were scattered around the property. And then five o'clock hit. The bike riders would be arriving any minute to a swarm of approximately 150 to 200 people. But it didn't stop there. From 6:00 to 8:00 p.m., Christian musicians Derrick Webb and Matthew Perryman Jones sang, bringing our total to roughly 600 people. Thank God the fire marshal didn't come!*

*It was survival mode. I had seven or eight people behind the counter. We couldn't keep up with anything! My mind shouted, "Ahhhhhh!" as I ran around, getting drinks out, filling supplies, hanging mugs, and making the occasional run back to our supply store in downtown Nashville. I had already been there every day this week, but that didn't stop me from making at least two more trips during the block party alone.*

*"We're almost out of ice again!" I'd hear a barista say, prompting me to make my recurring dash to the little gas station on the corner, for what added up to thirty bags of ice.*

---

[19] Blood:Water Mission: http://www.bloodwater.org/

*There was nowhere to sit. Nowhere to stand. Nowhere to park. Nowhere to even drive. People covered every inch of The Well's parking lot. News channels came to cover the story, videotaping all the action at this new Green Hills coffee house.*

* * *

*It wasn't until I walked into The Well the following Monday morning that it finally hit me. Wow … this isn't a dream! We are open. Our huge event is over and customers are still coming through our door. In that moment I knew …* this was going to work.

*That week, my wife and I took the time to pray, thanking God for everything He had done. He deserved all of the glory.*

## Just Beginning (Rob)

During that first week, we sold more coffee and merchandise than was needed to cover our first month's rent. Throughout the month and a half that followed, we were featured or highlighted on all local news stations, newspapers, magazines, and countless blogs. Customers raved about our decor and coffee. A quick glance at our twitter feed displayed hundreds of happy customers, deeming us, "The best cup of coffee in town," or "My new favorite place in Nashville." The Well had even sponsored its first project, purchasing a washing machine for a very poor infirmary in Morant Bay, Jamaica. We had pulled it off, springing from the starting blocks into a full-fledged sprint!

Three weeks after opening, The Wishing Well made a huge connection. Jessica, a young lady in her early twenties, posted to the wall: "I've just moved here from Oregon. I need a way to get around but can't even find a job because I have no transportation." Days later, Tristan, a young man in his mid-twenties, peered at the wall. He had been praying for God to show him how to make a difference in the world through being sacrificial. Jessica's need leapt toward him. He pulled the square card from the board and slipped it in his pocket.

"Hi, Jessica? My name is Tristan. I read your need that you left on the Wishing Well at The Well Coffeehouse. And well, I have a truck I want to give you," he said.

Such a powerful exchange—but the generosity didn't stop there. Our customers continue to take care of each other every single day.

Looking back, I had no idea that this was only a small step forward. The Well was an every-day platform—a marketplace for people to come, Christians and non-Christians alike; a way for us to love them through our service, through our Wishing Well, through our interactions. And now that we had pulled off a successful phase one, I could now get excited about phase two.

* * *

After the first five months of being open for business, I had come to the conclusion that God was leading me toward the next goal: planting a church within The Well. It was as if I could hear Him saying, "Okay, you've had success with the coffee house. Now it's time to take the next step."

Every day I would walk in envisioning what would take place. This church would look very different. We would worship, commune, and teach conversationally. It would be a living-room style church—a "house-church"—as if The Well were coming to *your* home personally.

Aimee and I prayed for guidance, knowing this was going to change our lives immensely. It wasn't just about one church within a coffee house—I wanted to open coffee houses across the country, planting churches in *all* of them. It would be called Well House, a network of churches. After establishing the first location, Chris and I would personally train and equip others to do the same in other locations. But how could I start a church and still support my family, especially with a very small group in attendance? I had no idea. Finally I concluded to Aimee, "Okay, if we feel led to do this, it's time to step out on faith."

> **"Don't try to grow a church. Try to BLESS A CITY.**
> **If you do, God will grow His Church."**
> ~Mark Batterson

While bringing The Well Coffeehouse to life, I had been supported financially by my current youth-minister position. Now, realizing I would most likely have to leave that position behind, also knowing my salary wouldn't come from The Well, my wife and I continued to pray for financial guidance.

"Why don't you see if our church will go in on Well House with you? Maybe they could keep you on staff and place you in the position to plant churches the same way they have placed missionaries in Africa?" Aimee suggested.

I loved the idea, but would they support me? Could we really do this together? There was only one way to find out.

In January, 2013, we held an Elders Ministers Retreat, meeting at Lipscomb University to discuss the church's goals and future plans. That Friday night, I sat amongst the team engaged in the topics and discussion. A small corner of my mind led me elsewhere—it was time to share my next steps for The Well. However, in that moment I would be alienating myself. The Tusculum family had been very supportive and appreciative of me during my past ten years. But my vision was more outside-the-box than what they would probably go for. And then there was that rising hesitation: Would the experience at my previous church happen again? Would they say, "No, *don't you know?* Church happens in a building! We don't think crazy like that."

I arrived home from the retreat at ten o'clock and crawled into bed. But sleep wasn't on the agenda. We were scheduled to meet again at 9:00 a.m., and I couldn't keep this information to myself any longer. I stayed up until 2:00 a.m., carefully crafting an e-mail to Michael*, one of our elders. The subject heading read: "Please open and read before we meet at 9:00 a.m." The body of the e-mail explained my plan to lead the new church, knowing I would probably have to step away from my career at Tusculum to do it. However, I also presented the question,

"Could we do this together? Could we explore the opportunity?" Before I could change my mind, my finger clicked Send.

At 8:00 a.m., my phone rang. "I *love* this, Rob. We have to share this with the rest of the guys today. Come ready to share. I'll tell you when it's time."

My senses heightened with exhilaration. He liked the plan! Yet, all day, my nerves spun, knowing the second I shared my intentions, things would change.

Lunch came to an end as Michael gave me the nudge. "Okay, when we go back, we're going to meet for about an hour to talk about some more church-related matters. Then I'd like you to share what's on your heart with the rest of the guys."

My stomach churned. Here we went.

All eyes were on me as I explained, "Guys, what I'm about to share with you is pretty heavy because it involves a major transition around here. I've been called to the mission field."

Eyebrows raised as I continued, "But that mission field is not overseas, it's right here in Nashville. God is calling me to plant churches."

As if starting a church within a coffee house wasn't forward thinking enough, I dropped the next bombshell. "I also feel led for this church to be instrumental."

Expressions froze. Though silence followed, the statement "you're kidding me" couldn't have been louder. In the churches in which I'd grown up and served in ministry, a cappella worship is a *sacred* tradition. This would be a large dividing factor in the decision making. Could they support a church that looked very different from them? I didn't know for sure. But I did know that they deserved every detail up front.

One of the elders stated, "We appreciate your boldness, Rob. Thank you for sharing this with us. We're going to meet separately to discuss if we could support you in your church-planting vision."

* * *

Three months passed while I waited on the verdict. During one of our routine Wednesday night meetings, the moment arrived. The elders asked a few more questions, allowing me to present my final case.

"Guys, I would love for you to support me on this, but I also know that this concept is very different. I'll respect your decision either way. Thank you for taking the time to consider it." I then left the room so they could deliberate.

The next morning I received the call.

An elder explained, "We love your passion, Rob. We love your strategy to plant churches. But if it's going to be instrumental, we can't support it. We honestly feel that it may cause division within our church. We want what's best for you and will support you. You can stay on staff as long as you would like. We also give you the freedom to change your mind because we would love for you to stay another twenty years here."

But I wasn't going to change my mind. Their willingness to keep me on staff was a very gracious offer, but God was calling me to lead this church, and to do so instrumentally. I laid down my salary, respectfully parting ways during the following six months. I was walking into the unknown, as we had when deciding to initially open The Well, only in a different way. A great way.

Most people got on board with a mission to open a coffee house in support of the poverty stricken. But to pioneer planting a church within a coffee house, challenging the religious system? That was debatable, with a surplus of questions attached. Some thought I had lost my way. But that was okay. My goal wasn't to please anyone. Aimee and I shared a passion to reach people who didn't know Jesus. But in order to do that, we needed to reach outside of the institution. We walked out of something that was familiar and safe, onto a glorious blank canvas. God never said, "Here's how it works," laying it all out there. But he *was* saying, "One step at a time—*do you trust me?*"

Our future wasn't filled with fear, but possibility.

> *"When nothing is sure, everything is possible."*
> *~Margaret Drabble*

## Thumped (Chris)

Nicki and I took a Sunday morning class in Oregon. Our teacher said, "When you're doing something right, Satan starts thumping you. He wants to distract you."

For example, when you're driving somewhere to do something positive and your car breaks down. You can't get to your location on time, if at all. You're getting thumped. This may happen more and more often the closer you get to a finish line.

While working toward The Well's opening, I had been presented with a few other job opportunities, always choosing to turn them down. However, after our Grand Opening, at a point where we had picked up a lot of momentum, I received a call from the district manager at a well-known retailer. After a two-hour interview and follow-up meeting, I was faced with the moment of truth. It came down to what was motivating my answer. Money and security? Or making a difference?

It wasn't a difficult decision. I knew what I wanted ... or rather what I didn't want. I wanted to be different. I wanted to have a positive effect on the world, not just take from it. I didn't want to return to a life without my wife and kids. An offer falling into my lap the moment The Well was starting to make a difference, again, couldn't have been a coincidence. I recognized that call for what it was—a distraction and not an opportunity. A temptation, not a calling. I was being thumped.

> **"If you don't build your dream someone will hire you to help build theirs."**
> ~Tony Gaskins

God brought us to Nashville for a reason. He guided our lives so that we were in the place He wanted, at the time we needed to be there. I believe he does that with everybody and everything. But we don't only have one option, one big opportunity to jump and follow God's Will. He provides a lot of different options. It's just a matter of asking ourselves—are we open to it?

*We've been lifted up and carried along this road. We couldn't have done any of this on our own. Every step of the way we could have been shut down. And every time, He had an answer for us—a cracked door waiting to be swung open. The key was seeking and following what He wanted, not what we planned.*

> **"In their hearts humans plan their course,**
> **but the LORD establishes their steps."**
> Proverbs 16:9
> (NIV)

## Walk on Water (Rob)

In September, 2013, Well House had a successful launch! We teach the gospel in a non-legalistic, non-judgmental way. That doesn't mean we water-down truth or dodge certain issues. But I believe there is a way to present the gospel where you're loving people into the kingdom. I speak about Jesus in a way that many customers have never heard before—not as a Jesus who has come to condemn, but about a Jesus who loves you so much that nothing could ever separate you from that love. We hope to build a community that is almost irresistibly loving, not crafting Jesus into something He's not, but presenting Him in His most organic form, which I believe *is* irresistible.

After being welcomed into Well House, nine people have come to know Jesus who would have never entered a church building. They consist of atheists, agnostics, a young man practicing Sikhism (an Indian religion), a woman contemplating suicide, and a family on the verge of homelessness. In addition, many more who had been alienated from the church have now found a home with us each week. This is why I do what I do.

\* \* \*

We've already built wells in Togo, Kenya, and Haiti. But that's just the beginning. We want to build thousands all over the world, wherever there is a need. When people buy our coffee, they are fighting poverty. They are invited into a bigger story, and they don't even necessarily know it.

This is what I was put on earth to do. God's plans often take us through pain in order to teach us to trust. I can't imagine what I would have missed had I somehow stayed at the church that fired me. And now, here I go again. This time I left a church by my own choosing, heading into the unknown to plant churches that are inclusive and embracing. God is filling The Well, one cup, one person at a time.

> **"It never works out like it's planned,
> but it always works out like it should."**
> ~Nancy Witt Adams

\* \* \*

A teenager in my youth group once told me, "You've taught us a lot of lessons, but the biggest lesson has been what you're doing at The Well. If He can use you to do this, having absolutely no business experience, then I'm just excited about how He can use me."

The Well has given us a way to model putting faith into action. Not that we're doing it perfectly, because we're not. We don't have it all figured out. We are simply modeling what anyone is capable of doing. So in 2009, I began assigning an annual project to my *The Story of the Church* class at Lipscomb University. I challenge my students with the question, "If you were to plant a church in the twenty-first century, what would that look like?" Each year, the responses are packed with insight and inspiration. I can't wait for the world to see them unfold.

\* \* \*

It takes courage to step out there when God calls us, just as it took courage for Peter to get out of the boat and walk on water toward Jesus in the middle of a storm. Peter wanted to walk out to Him, but he had to believe that he could step on that water. Like Peter, we had to get out of the boat, get our feet wet, and trust that He would secure each of our steps.

> **"Shortly before dawn Jesus went out to them, walking on the lake. When the disciples saw him walking on the lake, they were terrified. 'It's a ghost,' they said, and cried out in fear. But Jesus immediately said to them: 'Take courage! It is I. Don't be afraid.' 'Lord, if it's you,' Peter replied, 'tell me to come to you on the water.' 'Come,' he said. Then Peter got down out of the boat, walked on the water and came toward Jesus. But when he saw the wind, he was afraid and, beginning to sink, cried out, 'Lord, save me!' Immediately Jesus reached out his hand and caught him. 'You of little faith,' he said, 'why did you doubt?'"**
> *Matthew 14:25-31*
> *(NIV)*

But from time to time, like Peter, I doubted and sank beneath the waves. Jesus says to us in these moments, "You of little faith, why did you doubt?" I think what he's asking isn't, "Why did you doubt me?" What he really wants to know is, why are we doubting ourselves? We begin focusing on the wind and waves, doubting our own abilities, and inevitably, our feet fall beneath the water line. Looking back at our journey, and all that is to come, the process becomes clear: We had to get out of the boat, listen to Jesus, and trust—not only in Him, but that he equipped all of us to walk on water.

---

*Names or locations have been changed to protect those involved.

Reflection Questions

1. Rob and Chris endured less-than-ideal experiences by others of the same or similar faith in God. After those occurrences, are you surprised they didn't fall away from God or their faith?

2. As we walk down each of our roads, a limb falls in the path, demanding a call to action. Do we step over the road blocks? Do we alter our courses and walk around? Or do we swiftly turn on our heels, heading back to where we began? The Well experienced a plethora of obstacles in its path. However, it was clear that God wanted the board to continually move forward. But is it ever okay to make a 180-degree turn? How will we know?

3. "Drawing circles" around our prayers is such a powerful and most likely novel concept. Have you ever "circled" your need or desire in prayer? How do you feel about making such a passionate stance?

4. Is there something you think you are called to do? Is there an urge deep within, begging you to step out of the boat? What is holding you back?

# Irresistible Love: Seeds of Growth

*"You will seek me and find me when you
seek me with all your heart."*
Jeremiah 29:13
(NIV)

Be still.

Building The Well was beyond complicated. Beyond risky. Beyond exhausting. The board had a hundred moving parts to research, coordinate, and monitor. Chris spoke of The Well team "struggling for a way to get through—to make things work." In hindsight, it was evident that at times, when unsure of where to turn, they attempted to "force perceptions and ideas." However, the most progress was made when slowing their strides, simply listening to God's voice. Something inside would whisper, "What about this?"

Imagine how much progress could be accomplished if we removed ourselves as road-blocks. We are so accustomed to running a constant sprint that the concept of slowing down to listen appears foreign and counter-productive. Yet at times, it truly is okay—*okay to just be.* To retract yourself from the daily grind. To clear your mind. To reconnect. Not only with yourself, but with God. That's when we achieve clarity—when we clear out the clutter.

\* \* \*

To know God exists is one thing, but to actually choose to follow Him is another. To know that He is in control is astute, but to choose to fully let go of that control is progress. We can choose to live with or without God, fully surrendering our control or struggling

184

to maintain our grasp. Though, regardless of that decision, you will continue to have a Heavenly Father who loves you more than you could ever fathom. He is by your side at this very moment. He wants nothing more than to spend time with you. To remove the weight from your back. To lead you on your journey.

However, choosing to live a life with God does not mean engaging in a one-sided relationship. Start the conversation. Speak freely about your day. Confide in Him. He wants to know every part of you. He wants to hear your requests and concerns. But it can't end there. Seek Him. Be still. Let His presence envelop you. Dig deeper. Read the Word and listen intently to hear His answers. Be consistent.

> *"Every morning I spend fifteen minutes filling my mind full of God; And so there's no room left for worry or thoughts."*
> ~Howard Chandler Christy

This is where confidence is bolstered. Not just personal confidence or confidence in the future, but confidence in God and your relationship with Him. Make time today for these moments. Give your conversations the same level of attention that you would grant a dear friend whom you haven't seen in ages. The clarity and restoration that results from this indescribable connection with God is immeasurable.

> *"Be still, and know that I am God;"*
> Psalm 46:10
> (NIV)

# CHAPTER 8

## Bridging the Gap

*"God wastes nothing in our lives. Things meant*
*for evil are used for good results."*
~Bruce Atchison

A s I drank in the personal experiences that have so heavily shaped the lives of these men and women, I experienced a myriad of emotions. First and foremost, honor. To the majority of these individuals, I was a stranger about to become a confidant, with nothing but intuition telling them to have a little faith in me. Their life-changing stories were being disclosed by this wide-eyed woman. Moments that can be challenging to reflect upon, let alone describe in detail.

*"A bird doesn't sing because it has an answer.*
*It sings because it has a song."*
~Maya Angelou

You may be thinking, *what does my life have to do with theirs? I have my own responsibilities, priorities, and constraints. You don't know me. You don't get it.* Not only may your conditions not mirror theirs, but each testimony itself was unto its own. Family design/upbringing, geographical location(s), education, support systems, the experience(s) themselves, and relationships with God varied between and throughout each story. But are there underlying commonalities? We may not all struggle with addiction to alcohol or drugs, but what about addiction to success, food, social media, or even worrying? You may not have lost a house or job in a natural disaster, but you may have lost one due to a recession or unemployment. Perhaps you have yet to cope with the loss of a loved one, but lately, you're feeling so lost and alone it's as if you had.

*Gap (noun): a break in a barrier; a separation*
*in space; an incomplete or deficient area*
*(Merriam-Webster, 2015)*

Yet, a gap still lies before us. Though similarities exist, there is an obvious discrepancy between one person's experiences and those of the other thousand people they pass on the street. However, finding the application of another's stepping stones within our own lives, without having to live each experience, can be a gift in and of itself. How exhausting would it be if we were expected to personally experience and absorb each and every life lesson? Think about that for a moment. It would be unbearable. Instead, we can appreciate this gap—not only recognizing a necessary compassion for others, but also the opportunity it provides toward personal growth.

Moreover, what about our common gaps? The gap between stress and freedom from burden? The gap between good intentions and the realization of our actions? The gap between what we hunger for and what will actually satisfy? We experience these battles each and every day. Different settings. Common struggles.

## Common Stones

The words of wisdom on the upcoming page came directly from the six courageous men and women who contributed to this book. While each account holds great merit, I won't pretend that their documented stepping stones provide a thorough map of answers. I won't adhere to the notion that this is all you will need in order to conquer a mountain or make progress in your relationship with God. But I do know that experiencing a connection to another's life is a gift beyond words. Individually, our experiences may seem continents apart, but perhaps the ripple from another's wave will encourage your boat to sail a little farther.

*"Then, by the will of God, I will be able to come to you with a joyful heart, and we will be an encouragement to each other."*
*Romans 15:32*
*(NLT)*

*~Notice the miracles.*

*~Let God hold you up.*

*~Don't underestimate the ordinary.*

*~Move past what you cannot change.*

*~Don't try to control the chaos. Let go.*

*~Indulge in The Word. Let it lead you.*

*~Even when no one is looking, do what is right.*

*~Forgive. Bitterness won't change the end result.*

*~Honor your responsibilities. Live up to your word.*

*~Strive for inclusion, embracing those who are different.*

*~Ask God for what you need. Don't expect Him to know.*

*~Do what you love. Put a bit of you into everything you do.*

*~Celebrate the milestones, no matter how big or how small.*

*~Stop doubting yourself. Get out of the boat. Walk on water.*

*~Don't fear history–you'll only be living it over again each and every day.*

*~Enjoy what you have. You can always find something to be thankful for.*

*~Use your talents to give back. Reach out to those in need. Make your life count.*

*~Lean on and appreciate friends and family. Those connections cannot be replaced.*

*~Build a personal relationship with God. Appreciate His grace, guidance, and protection ... even His humor.*

*~Don't be afraid to do things differently, opening your mind to larger horizons.*

*~Listen intently. Strive to follow God's instruction, not solely searching for your own answers.*

*~If you won't continue the fight for yourself, continue the fight for those whom you love.*

Do common stepping stones exist? Aside from the reliable take-homes on the previous page, are there common denominators between each of these testimonies? What pulls us away from what may seem to be ceaseless trials? Hard work? Unquestionably. A positive attitude? Absolutely. A friendly hand? Without a doubt. A lot of our stones are similar, and yet, some are crafted unto us alone. I was blown away by Ben, Kathy, Chappy, Penny, Rob, and Chris. Blown away by their transparency, by their humility, by their strength, but most importantly, by their faith. Faith in themselves. Faith in tomorrow. Faith in God.

> **"Now faith is the substance of things hoped**
> **for, the evidence of things not seen."**
> *Hebrews 11:1*
> *(KJV)*

Faith. Our common stone. When I started this journey, I knew faith would play a role, though I had no idea to what extent. Finding security in something or someone that cannot be assured without a doubt is a battle in and of itself. Maintaining that faith during the ups and downs can be even more of a challenge. Even aside from our personal lives, we are constantly bombarded with events on the evening news that would leave anyone wondering why. *Why did this have to happen? Where are you, God? How much more can You expect us to take? When is enough, enough?*

At times, I have struggled with these uncertainties as well. However, I eventually realized we may be asking the wrong questions. Perhaps the question isn't where is God? He's here. He's always been here. But rather, to what extent have we let God into our lives? Is our focus continually on what He hasn't done for us, as opposed to what we could do for Him? Are we putting in the work, or instead, always looking for the easy way out? Are we focusing on His wisdom and power as if He is in fact enough? Herein lies another gap—the gap between the main attraction, and its competing distractions.

> **"When you keep getting the wrong answers,**
> **try asking better questions."**
> ~Jonathan Lockwood Huie

## What's Your Angle?

To acquire the snapshot introducing this chapter, I walked around the massive cross with a purpose. Breathing in the fresh mountain air, I gazed down from the peak I stood upon at the sprawling lake below, letting myself escape into the serenity within that moment. A prime photo opportunity was in my midst; I just had to find it—and do so quickly. The weathermen had predicted reoccurring showers the entire week, and the clouds hovering over my head supported the day's forecast. A moist scent of rain approached, warning me of its impending arrival. Yet, despite these subtle threats, I had a job to do.

I'm an amateur photographer at best, but that didn't mean I wouldn't put some sweat into obtaining a decent finished product. *Maybe if I move a little to the right. Nope. Perhaps downward and to the left?* As I engaged in an annoying game of hide and seek with the remaining light, my patience dwindled with every click from my camera. Approximately two dozen pictures later, attempting a dozen different angles and focal points, I was very close to throwing in the towel in an effort to escape the impending downpour. *There's always tomorrow. Maybe I should just come back.* Nah ... I was close. Too close to give up, even if it meant getting a bit uncomfortable.

Time to dive in—or *down*, rather. There I was, flat on my back, wiggling around in the dirt and rocks as several kids stood nearby wondering who this crazy person was and why she would subject herself to rolling around on the ground for a measly picture. *Ignore that stone penetrating your skull, Alicia. Focus.* My shutter flashed. That was it! That was the one. Somehow within the haze I found what I needed as the sun momentarily beamed through a pocket of clouds directly upon the object of my affection. I walked away in satisfaction as the rain drops gradually kissed my forehead. Just in time.

\* \* \*

Seeing God and really understanding His purpose in this world is similar to acquiring a "perfect" snapshot. Sometimes we have to get nice and dirty. It can be painful. Often we have to withstand frustration, desperately clinging to every ounce of patience remaining. We may have to approach the situation from dozens of different angles and perspectives before we find the right one. Before we find truth. Before we find the light. We have to trust that what we need is there, even amidst the haze. And in the end, only with Him will we be saved from the rain.

> **"For our light and momentary troubles are achieving for us an eternal glory that far outweighs them all."**
> 2 Corinthians 4:17
> (NIV)

I've doubted God. I've scraped bottom and wondered if it was easier to tackle my issues on my own. Then it hit me … I'm on the bottom *because* I tried to do it on my own. I had been sitting by, idly waiting for God to notice me, while he had been waiting for the signal that I was ready to trust Him. That I would listen this time. That I would surrender.

I was the one who needed to shift. While I was so obstinate in claiming God had abandoned me in my time of need, how was I actually *letting Him* take control? I thought I knew how my life should go, and God was helping as long as I agreed with how the chess pieces were moving. And in those moments where I was listening for some type of message from the heavens, how could I possibly hear His guidance if I wasn't reading His words? I was a hypocrite. I wasn't listening … I was demanding.

# Clarity

## MOST Ministries Eyeglass Clinic
### Alicia's Journal Entry
### Nicaragua; July 21, 2003

*Hola, God. What an amazing day! We worked our booties off, fitting a total of 320 Nicaraguans with eyeglasses, putting in an extra three hours to finish seventy people above our quota. Our team experienced a lot of life-changing moments, to say the least.*

*It's indescribably uplifting, the moment when you hold up the testing lenses and the patient finally exclaims, "I can see!" It takes your breath away, bringing immediate tears to your eyes. What a blessing to be able to play a role—any role—in this miracle.*

*One man with extremely poor eyesight (all signs pointed to cataracts) came to my station. We began assessing his near-sighted vision capabilities (or lack thereof). I did my best to assist him, but realizing it was pretty much out of my hands, I turned to my team member, Steve, asking him to pray with us. With the help of our translator, Ernesto, the four of us prayed together, leaving it in God's hands. It crushed me to have to turn away someone in need.*

*Later in the day, I came across the extreme prescription (amongst our collection of donated, used eyeglasses) that I had needed for this man. I ran through the clinic until I found him, believing I could still provide some clarity despite his condition.*

*The lenses I had found were correct (or as close as I could possibly get to the prescription strength that his eyes demanded). They were able to provide some clarity in a world full of fog.*

*It's so easy to take clear vision for granted.*

In our moments of clarity, our lenses are sharpened, providing the realization that God is more than just this figure in the sky. But in the interim lies the struggle. We will all encounter a series of challenges that test our beliefs, our strengths, and our abilities. So often we get angry and blame God for our circumstances and pitfalls. At times, in the face of adversity, it can even feel as if He is nowhere to be found.

> **"God enters by a private door into every individual."**
> ~Ralph Waldo Emerson

God knows exactly how to approach us—exactly what prescription lens will bring all of our daily curve balls into focus, exactly what strings will strike a chord within our hearts. In photography we pursue life. We follow the light. We chase meaningful perspectives. As when taking a photo, a new perspective can allow us to see God, understand God, or learn to trust Him. This new lens can bend the light directly in a way that no human could devise or recreate. This focused light eliminates the blur: negativity—doubt, blame, anger, and a million other self-defeating elements.

> **"In order for the light to shine so brightly,
> the darkness must be present."**
> ~Francis Bacon

Adversity was never God's plan for our lives. Satan uses our freedom of choice to bring about a world of sin. However, it's easy to forget that God didn't intend for our pain to exist, and yet it's *because* of God that we rise up and have a future. A future that grows sharper the moment we allow His light to pass through our prescriptive lens, designed by Him alone. God created every single molecular cell within our bodies, as well as the very ground upon which we stand. How can we honestly believe that He does not know better than we do?

> **"But Job replied, '... Should we accept only good things**
> **from the hand of God and never anything bad?' ..."**
> *Job 2:10*
> *(NLT)*

In everything we do and encounter, the purest light focuses not on the obstacle, but on how to *overcome* the obstacle. *What is the lesson that will benefit my life? Is God shielding me from a larger issue?* If the situation is approached in this manner, wisdom is apt to follow. God does in fact have a plan. But that doesn't mean that we aren't expected to make powerful assessments and choices. Each choice that we make, following God's instruction, is a tool in motion, intended to achieve the big picture: God's work. His photography. His portfolio. It's an honor to play a role.

> **"If any of you lacks wisdom, you should ask God,**
> **who gives generously to all without finding**
> **fault, and it will be given to you."**
> *James 1:5*
> *(NIV)*

## Embrace the Waves

> **Embrace (verb): to avail oneself of**
> *(Merriam-Webster, 2015)*

Unforeseen challenges and calamities will occur, no matter how much we attempt to remain in control. If you tie your boat tightly to the dock, it may prevent wreckage from the occasional storm, but also only allows you to absorb the scenery and experiences surrounding the shore. And frankly, even if one's fierce grip never loosens from perceived safety, swells or currents are never far from reach. So perhaps you decide to unravel the knots and take your chances. Each plummeting wave and destructive storm can teach you how to avoid injury, foresee potential collisions, and withstand the pressure. Through forced destruction, they cultivate strength. Through fear or doubt, they instill valor. Through devastation, they teach us not only how to survive, but how to prevail.

*"Consider it pure joy, my brothers and sisters, whenever you face trials of many kinds, because you know that the testing of your faith produces perseverance. Let perseverance finish its work so that you may be mature and complete, not lacking anything."*
*James 1:2-4*
*(NIV)*

Rough waters shape us. They improve upon the people we are. They give life purpose. They remind us to have gratitude for what we've been given. After all, the sun's warmth is always more appreciated after hiding for days. These waters not only teach us what faith is, but how to develop that faith. God is in those waves—pulling meaning from adversity, producing calm if permitted, and anchoring when the likelihood of capsizing becomes great. I have always deemed it silly to search for a "sole purpose" in life (truly believing we have many). However, perhaps said search isn't as fruitless as I once believed. Our purpose may be to embrace the waves, unyielding in our determination to become someone better than our present selves. To allow His strength and love to shine through our fight.

*"Later that night, the boat was in the middle of the lake, and he was alone on land. He saw the disciples straining at the oars, because the wind was against them. Shortly before dawn he went out to them, walking on the lake. He was about to pass by them, but when they saw him walking on the lake, they thought he was a ghost. They cried out, because they all saw him and were terrified. Immediately he spoke to them and said, 'Take courage! It is I. Don't be afraid.'"*
*Mark 6:47-50*
*(NIV)*

Lessons are paramount. However, what can be overlooked is the importance of accepting the storm itself—not just holding on tight, but embracing our roles and valuing their purpose, as difficult and callous as that may seem. This is not to say that we should seek rough waters, nor is it a disregard or belittlement of any resulting fear or despondency. The situations we experience are often a result of our choices. Other times the situation happened *to* us, making us victims of circumstance. Either way, we have a strong hand in changing the tide. We have a choice. Embrace that choice. First let yourself process the doubt, fear, and pain. But then embrace the opportunity to turn your situation around. Embrace the opportunity for greatness, despite the circumstance.

> **"Challenges are gifts that force us to search for a new center of gravity. Don't fight them. Just find a different way to stand."**
> ~Xai

An experience doesn't have to be extraordinary to produce a valuable lesson. Hundreds of important lessons surround us in our sometimes mundane daily routines. While each stepping stone of progress assists toward guiding us in the right direction, some stones are more crucial than others. We may even mistakenly give one stone more credit than it deserves, overlooking the sturdy, enduring rock that has proved itself to be the foundation for them all. Our faith is that foundation. God is our single, ever-present rock. He is the common stone that surfaced again and again in each of these testimonies—not just as an encouraging force, but as The Leg on which to stand, knowing ours alone are feeble.

> **"But in your hearts revere Christ as Lord. Always be prepared to give an answer to everyone who asks you to give the reason for the hope that you have. But do this with gentleness and respect,"**
> 1 Peter 3:15
> (NIV)

# Rest in Safety

> **Bridge (noun): a structure carrying a pathway**
> **or roadway over a depression or obstacle**
> *(Merriam-Webster, 2015)*

We may never be able to determine the "why" behind each of our experiences, but perhaps not needing to know "why" is the true accomplishment. Does our reasoning truly matter? Or does our trust in the One Constant overrule the confusion and doubt? Do we really need to struggle for control over the reins? Or does comfort come with never needing to concern ourselves with the master plan, crafted by our wise Heavenly Father who is *always* in our corner?

*He* is our bridge. He is the bridge between misery and comfort. Our bridge between insecurity and confidence. Our bridge between doubt and certainty. He is our bridge between despair and hope. Ultimately, despite any logical reasoning conjured up to explain life's events, our lives designed by God are more extraordinary than our own designs could ever be.

> *"If you direct your heart rightly, you will*
> *stretch out your hands toward him.*
> *If iniquity is in your hand, put it far away, and do*
> *not let wickedness reside in your tents.*
> *Surely then you will lift up your face without*
> *blemish; you will be secure and will not fear.*
> *You will forget your misery; you will remember*
> *it as waters that have passed away.*
> *And your life will be brighter than the noonday;*
> *its darkness will be like the morning.*
> *And you will have confidence, because there is hope;*
> *you will be protected and take your rest in safety."*
> *Job 11:13-18*
> *(NRSV)*

# CHAPTER 9

## Conclusion ~ Your Choice

*"We all make choices, but in the end our choices make us."*
~Ken Levine

The lobby of the movie theater was surprisingly empty for a Friday night. At the ticket counter I paused, struggling to remember the name of the movie that I had somehow convinced my angelic husband to attend. The attendant behind the counter gazed vacantly toward the parking lot, desperately awaiting life beyond the glass between us. Finally giving up on my fruitless hunt, I asked, "May I please have two tickets to the movie with the little boy who has leaves growing out of his legs?"

She laughed and handed me two tickets to *The Odd Life of Timothy Green*.

I knew very little about this film. For some strange reason, I just assumed it would be an inspiring, feel-good movie, prompting my need to indulge. However, during the first five minutes it became apparent that my expectations were inaccurate. I believe Ryan's words were "self-inflicted torture."

Not to say that the movie was awful. I enjoyed it. However, given our current circumstances, its foundational context wasn't what we wanted to build our Friday night upon. The couple in the movie couldn't have children. Physically couldn't. They had attempted to the nth degree, resulting in disappointment after disappointment. The doctors concurred that another road aside from natural conception must be considered (adoption, surrogacy, a gestational carrier, etc.).

Within the past six to eight months, Ryan and I had endured a similar battle. By no means was getting pregnant and carrying our child impossible. However, I had a handful of anatomical anomalies that predicted a difficult road. Ryan and I strapped on our brave faces months ago, but somewhere deep within lay more fear and sadness than we cared to admit. During the movie, I attempted desperately not to stare with envy at the little girl to our left crawling onto her father's lap to cuddle—her blonde ponytail swinging from her delight.

After several buckets of both popcorn and tears, I glared at the ending credits like a statue. Ryan slowly peered over at me (probably plotting how to get even).

"I have no idea what to do with that," I said, followed by a flight of nervous laughter.

Obviously the movie wasn't requesting anything of me. But *I was*.

\* \* \*

Two years later. With countless procedures and even surgery behind us, Ryan and I remained childless, continuing to fight that same, haunting battle. My days were suffocated by constant aches, sporadic pills and injections, a rigid diet, and doctor's appointments that were anything but comforting. Those visits became routine—as typical as pulling over to fill my gas tank once or twice a week.

"I'm falling apart, Ryan. This is a constant game of pain, physically and mentally. We pace in anticipation of each test result, never able to plan for the future given that each verdict controls tomorrow. All the while resisting resentment toward couples that have babies and never even wanted them! And really, I find myself wondering … in all of this … am I even *living* anymore?" I confessed.

I had lost faith—not in God, but in myself. What I lacked, I couldn't obtain. I couldn't just build a skill, work harder, or plan my time more wisely. Physically, I didn't and couldn't "measure up."

> **"We don't get to choose what is true. We only**
> **get to choose what we do about it."**
> *~Kami Garcia*

On a chilly, February morning, my head finally surfaced above the rushing waters. *We aren't without options. I lose if I stand still.*

There are *always* opportunities ... and there is *always* a choice to seek light beyond the darkness.

\* \* \*

Sometimes you don't want to be strong. You've been fighting for so long you've forgotten why you chose that path in the first place. The current battle may not be the same as the last, but yet, one runs into the next —a revolving door of trials. Perhaps you feel as if you aren't even living while in your continuous state of struggle and confusion. *Life can't be a constant trampling. Life isn't meant to be this heavy. Life can't be this .... Can it?*

> **"He gives power to the faint, and to him who**
> **has no might he increases strength."**
> *Isaiah 40:29*
> *(ESV)*

Here is where I argue that this is one of our closest states *to* living. You have been knocked around. You've gotten into that ring so many times that it now masquerades itself as a waste of time. The moment has arrived to make the decision: Force your arms up for the hundredth time or withdraw in defeat. But the minute you stop getting up, the minute you leave that ring by choice, the minute you are no longer fighting for what's good—fighting for your and His purpose—life has ceased.

> **"Victory is always possible for the person
> who refuses to stop fighting."**
> ~Napoleon Hill

Anyone can cruise through the good times, soar through the days that require nothing of your body or your will within. But when it's not easy, when you feel the pain of the stampede and exhaustion in your feeble limbs as they strive to stand just one more time: Stand. Do it again. And again and again. By choosing not to, you welcome loss. *The win is in the decision, the recognition of what's good and honorable.* And in that raw, vulnerable moment of choice, you have an opportunity at your fingertips. A turning point possibly determining a significant portion of your future, due to planting the seed of a single choice. How could you possibly *live* more than that?

This next moment is yours. Seize it.

Reflection Questions

1.  Did one of these testimonies resonate within you more than the others? Why?

2.  Where do you stand in your relationship with God? Is it beneficial to be "content" with the state of that relationship?

3.  After reading this last chapter, where do your thoughts and emotions lie? Right here, right now, pray about them. If you're not ready to cross that bridge, talk to someone you trust. Just don't ignore them. They exist for a reason.

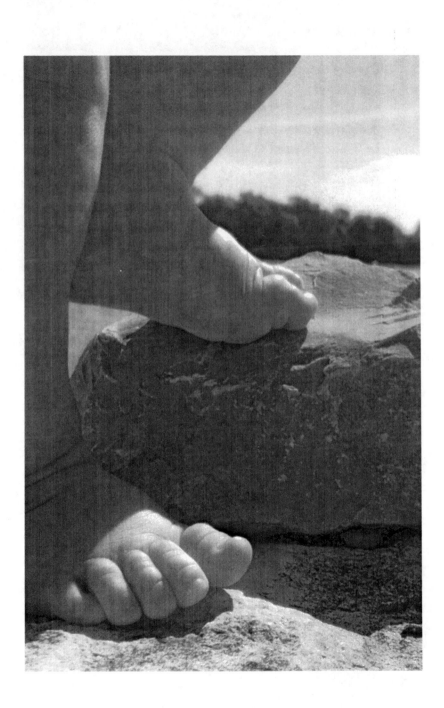

# CHAPTER 10

## Your Steps

*"I read and walked for miles at night along the
beach ... searching endlessly for someone wonderful who
would step out of the darkness and change my life. It
never crossed my mind that that person could be me."*
~Anna Quindlen

*T*ake the time to tell *your* story. Put your dreams, experiences, fears, struggles and triumphs on paper. Writing your thoughts down can provide a therapeutic release, recognizing an internal dialogue begging to be acknowledged.

*"We don't receive wisdom; we must discover it for ourselves
after a journey that no one can take for us or spare us."*
~Marcel Proust

Occasionally, we may be waiting for that unseen hero to enter our lives. This hero can be represented in a multitude of ways. Whether it be a person, an ideal job, or an opportunity of some sort, it can become easy to remain static in our discomfort, believing foolishly that someone or something other than ourselves and God must be present in order to pull us through. When in reality, with every progressive movement, we are our own advocates for success. At this moment, recognize the strength in *your* steps. You are stronger then you ever imagined.

*"Now to him who is able to do immeasurably more than all we ask or imagine, according to his power that is at work within us,"*
Ephesians 3:20
(NIV)


Pick up a pen, take a deep breath, and just ... *jump.*

_____

_____

_____

_____

_____

_____

_____

_____

_____

_____

_____

_____

_____

_____

_____

_____

_____

**"It's not forgetting that heals. It's remembering."**
~Amy Greene

# Your Steps
## (Continued)

_____

_____

_____

_____

_____

_____

_____

_____

_____

_____

_____

_____

_____

_____

_____

_____

_____

_____

_____

_____

_____

*"Every little thing you do matters; there is
no wasted effort in God's kingdom."*
~Author Unknown

# Your Steps
## (Continued)

_____

_____

_____

_____

_____

_____

_____

_____

_____

_____

_____

_____

_____

_____

_____

_____

_____

_____

_____

_____

_____

_____

*"What lies behind us and what lies before us are
tiny matters compared to what lies within us."*
*~Henry S. Haskins*

# Your Steps
## (Continued)

_____

_____

_____

_____

_____

_____

_____

_____

_____

_____

_____

_____

_____

_____

_____

_____

_____

_____

_____

_____

*"It's not who you are that holds you back,
it's who you think you're not."*
*~Author Unknown*

# *Your Steps*
## *(Continued)*

_____

_____

_____

_____

_____

_____

_____

_____

_____

_____

_____

_____

_____

_____

_____

_____

_____

_____

**"Let us work as if success depended upon ourselves alone;
but with heartfelt conviction that we are
doing nothing and God everything."**
~St. Ignatius Loyola

# ABOUT THE AUTHOR

Alicia M. Smith grew up in the suburbs of her beloved Detroit, MI, but in 2008, Nashville, TN, captured her heart. She resides there with her husband, Ryan, and ball-crazy Welsh corgi, Bagel. Though, wherever these two are—home truly is. Alicia is a writer and Special Project Consultant. She also enjoys blogging on topics revolving around finding calm (and God) in life's chaos. Her passion, simply put, is helping others ... in *any* capacity. Alicia empowers others to not only believe in their strength from within, but also the strength bestowed from above.

CPSIA information can be obtained at www.ICGtesting.com
Printed in the USA
LVOW10s0513101215

465798LV00003B/3/P